PHILADELPHIA DAILY
**NEWS**
*THE PEOPLE PAPER*

P R E S E N T S

# PHILADELPHIA'S GREATEST

# SPORTS

# MOMENTS

SPORTS PUBLISHING INC.
www.sportspublishinginc.com

**MIKE RATHET,** Executive Sports Editor

**PAT McLOONE,** Sports Editor

**MICHAEL MERCANTI,** Executive Photo Editor

◆

**CLAUDIA MITROI,** Coordinating Editor

**SUSAN M. McKINNEY,** Director of Production

**JENNIFER L. POLSON,** Interior Design, Senior Project Manager

**K. JEFFREY HIGGERSON,** Cover Design

**DAVID HAMBURG,** Copy Editor

ISBN 1-58382-059-0

Library of Congress Number 00-109732

Published by Sports Publishing Inc.

www.sportspublishinginc.com

# ACKNOWLEDGMENTS

Philadelphia, the City of Brotherly Love, as it has come to be known, has given sports fans such greats as Wilt Chamberlain, Mike Schmidt, Chuck Bednarik, Joe Frazier, Bernie Parent and many more. For every one of these stars' athletic feats, the Philadelphia Daily News has given its readers a front-row seat. When the Phillies won their first World Series, the *Daily News* was there. When Wilt scored 100 points, the Daily News was there, too.

Bringing these thrilling stories to life each day in the pages of the *Daily News* took the hard work and dedication of many people at the paper. While working on this project, we received the overwhelming support of Mike Rathet (Executive Sports Editor), Pat McLoone (Sports Editor), Michael Mercanti (Executive Photo Editor) and Helene Pierson. Among others at the paper who were instrumental in assisting us in this project were Ed Barkowitz, Bob Cooney, Bob Vetrone Jr., Mark Ludak and Ed Voves.

Space limitations preclude us from thanking all the writers and photographers whose contributions appear in this book. However, wherever available, we have preserved the writers' bylines and the photographers' credits to ensure proper attribution for their work.

Finally, I am grateful for all the support and effort of those at Sports Publishing Inc. who worked tirelessly on this project: Jennifer Polson, Joe Bannon Jr., Jeff Higgerson, Chris Cary, Kenny O'Brien and David Hamburg.

Claudia Mitroi
Coordinating Editor

# CONTENTS

# PHILADELPHIA'S GREATEST

## SPORTS MOMENTS

Mike Schmidt jumps on teammates celebrating Tug
McGraw's final pitch that clinched the 1980 World Series.
(Photo by Joe McLaughlin)

# A
# CENTURY OF
# BASEBALL

## BY BILL CONLIN

If you remember 1954, the year Connie Mack's sons, Roy, Earl and future U.S. senator from Florida, Connie Jr., sold the A's to Kansas City entrepreneur Arnold Johnson, you were middle-aged when the Phillies finally won a World Series.

Because most of the really horrible teams of the century have changed address or were replaced by expansion franchises, the Phillies stand alone as the losingest team in professional sports history. Those 8,200-plus losses have an almost epic quality, right down there with Germany's record in World Wars or Prince Albert of Monaco's international bobsledding record.

In his 50-year run, Connie Mack operated the A's out of a cigar box stuffed full of IOU's. Poverty forced Mack to sell off his great 1929-31 dynasty, thought by some to be the second-best team of all time behind the 1927 Yankees. In half a century, the A's never came close to drawing a million fans in an era when 500,000 paid admissions represented less than a dollar a head. When the Depression clamped down on Philadelphia, Mack couldn't spare a nickel, let alone a dime.

In 1943 Bob Carpenter scraped together $400,000 and handed the keys to his son. Thus began the Phillies' "Green Period." For the first time in the town's long and checkered baseball history, the city had an owner with deep pockets, the competitive instincts of an athlete and the money to match checkbooks with anybody.

The best move Carpenter made was to bring in Hall of Fame pitcher Herb Pennock in 1944 to be his general manager. The Whiz Kids, who outlasted the superior Dodgers in 1950, were built by Pennock, "The Squire of Kennett Square." Pennock became the first Phillies executive to enjoy an unfettered checkbook.

Pennock's nucleus was in place when he died in 1948. Carpenter became his own GM, eerily foreshadowing the disaster that befell Bill Giles in 1984, when he replaced Paul Owens, the best GM in franchise history, with himself.

By 1957, every team in the National League but the Phillies had signed at least one black player. The Phils signed John Kennedy, a light-hitting middle infielder who quietly was sent to the minors after a half cup of coffee.

Two years later, Bob Carpenter handcuffed himself to his desk and hired the penurious but talented John Quinn, a second-generation baseball lifer. He sent scout Dewey Griggs to scout an infielder named Ernie Banks. But Banks was injured and a kid named

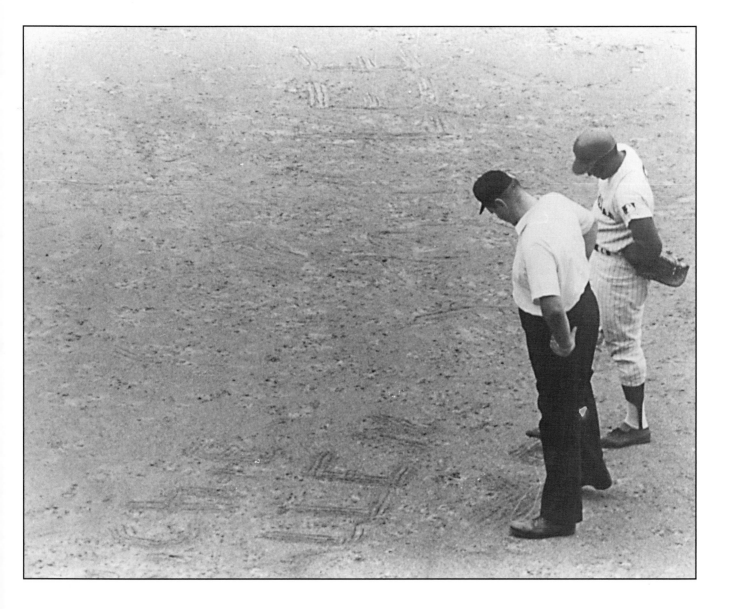

Richie Allen, always colorful and controversial with the
Phillies, uses his spikes to write messages on the infield dirt.
(Daily News photo by Sam Psoras)

Hank Aaron filled in at short. "Didn't get to see Banks," Griggs telegrammed Quinn, "but recommend we sign a boy named Aaron, who can really hit. Don't think he's a shortstop, though." For years, Quinn livened up cocktail parties with what the lineup would have been like with Banks and Aaron.

Gene Mauch, the handpicked manager who led the Phillies out of the wilderness of a 23-game losing streak in 1961, had the most ethnically mixed club in baseball. Not even the Dodgers had more African-American or Latin ballplayers: Rookie of the Year Dick Allen at third; Ruben Amaro platooning at short; Tony Taylor and Cookie Rojas sharing second base; Tony Gonzalez in center, with hulking former Braves slugger Wes Covington platooning in the outfield and young outfielders Johnny Briggs and Alex Johnson on the bench; first baseman Vic Power joining the Phils in September. It was not unusual for the '64 Phils to have six ballplayers of color in the lineup.

Quinn was kicked upstairs in 1972 after the Phils experienced another sickening plunge into last place, succeeded by a hard-living, middle-aged workaholic named Paul Owens. Owens was 6-4 and whippet lean. Allen nicknamed him "The Pope" for a resemblance to Pope Paul. This Pope didn't burn the candle at both ends; he melted it down. But he was all baseball man.

Carpenter had so much faith in Owens that he sent his son Ruly, a top Yale football and baseball player, to learn the art of the organization at the feet of the master.

And when Owens wore the mantle of power, he hired Carpenter favorite Dallas Green to run what by then had become an elite farm system. "Two things in baseball are certain," rival farm directors would joke. "The sun rises in the East and two Phillies scouts will be at every high school game."

To suggestions of cronyism, Owens would snap, "I hired Dallas because he's done every other job in the system, because he's a Phillies guy and because he's the only SOB who can keep up with me and Hugh Alexander."

Alexander was hired as the Phillies' first special-assignment scout, and soon became a behind-the-scenes Svengali who acquired the unofficial title of Minister of Trade.

Giles, then the club's vice president, a marketing and promotions whiz, suggested that Carpenter should interview an obscure Dodgers third-base coach named Danny Ozark. Ozark was said to be an organizational genius with the strong, silent demeanor of manager Walter Alston.

The Wizard of Oze survived a player mutiny and a late '73 Owens fact-finding trip to become the most successful manager in organization history. Starting in 1975, the Phillies reeled off a club-record nine consecutive winning seasons. Ozark was manager for the first five, including back-to-back 101-victory seasons in 1976 and 1977.

It remained for Green, who replaced Ozark in September of 1979, to lash Hell's Team to the singular 1980 World Series title.

The best of all might have been the 1981 team. We will never know. When the first devastating baseball strike hit that summer, the Phillies already had found that elusive higher gear. "You could see in their eyes after the strike they had lost it," Green said. "I never got them back. We had to go through that split [bleep]-season playoff thing and . . ."

And the club was for sale. The Carpenters smelled the winds of fiscal change in spring training and decided to fold their hand.

The Phillies have faded like a low-budget movie scene.

---

Mule Haas hit a three-run home run during a 10-run seventh inning as the Athletics overcame an 8-0 Cubs lead to capture Game 4 of the World Series on Oct. 12, 1929. Two days later, the A's scored three runs in the bottom of the ninth to overcome a 2-0 deficit and win the series, 4 games to 1.

Phillies outfielder Johnny Callison's three-run home run in the bottom of the ninth inning lifted the National League to a 7-4 All-Star Game win at Shea Stadium, July 7, 1964.

Even Ernie ("Let's play two!") Banks may not have stuck around for the completion of the Phillies-Padres doubleheader that started on July 2, 1993, and ended after 4 a.m., July 3, on an RBI single by relief pitcher Mitch Williams. It was Mitch's third—and final—hit of his 11-year major league career.

The 1950 Philadelphia Phillies surround their grateful manager, Eddie Sawyer (arms outstretched), as they celebrate their 4-1 victory over the Brooklyn Dodgers. The Phils took the National League pennant for the first time in 35 years. (Photo from The Philadelphia Inquirer collection)

# SISLER, ASHBURN, ROBERTS STAR AS PHILS TAKE FLAG

OCTOBER 1, 1950
BY GRANT DOHERTY

Benny Bengough cried and Dick Sisler laughed; Manager Eddie Sawyer tried to talk to everyone at once and Robin Roberts fell exhausted to the stool in front of his locker. There was back-thumping and hand-shaking and at least 100 press and radio men interviewed everyone from owner Bob Carpenter to other press and radio men. All the tenseness was gone—tenseness that had been building up for 154 games—they could laugh again and sing again—it was over—they had beaten the Dodgers, 4-1—victory was theirs.

Victory—a word spelled with seven letters and a feeling so precious that the Whiz Kids said it over and over, slowly letting their tongues savor it like a heady wine. It was hard to believe that they had done it, but they had. Their young courage had shown as bright red as the crimson of their caps, and they had come through despite injuries and losses of players and the fact that everyone else had said over and over, "You can't do it—you'll blow it—the Dodgers are too strong for you and will beat you."

So the tears and laughter and babble of 100 voices and popping of 1,000 flashbulbs rolled themselves into one thing and became the sounds and sights of victory.

"Knew it all the time, wasn't worried at all," said Coach Cy Perkins, and then he uncrossed his fingers for the first time since the game had started.

"That Roberts is the greatest pitcher that ever breathed," was Andy Seminick's contribution.

"Most beautiful home run I ever saw," Dick Whitman enthused.

"Ba-ruther," from Ken Silvestri.

"Where did you get that arm," Russ Meyer asked Richie Ashburn and was answered with "Aw, I had it all the time."

A few were, of course, singled out for special congratulations—Roberts for his magnificent pitching job, Sisler for his homer, Ashburn for his throw from center field that nipped what would have been the winning Dodger run in the ninth and Stan Lopata for the aplomb with which he received Ashburn's throw and tagged the stunned Cal Abrams at the plate—but all were heroes. They were underdogs who had bared their fangs and refused to give up and had won, and now that they had, they were still a team and wanted to remain a team—the Phillies—the Whiz Kids—the 1950 National League champions.

Roberts was reluctant to talk about his spectacular pitching triumph. He grinned and accepted congratulations, but his only comment on the game itself was "I'm sure glad it turned out that way—it meant a lot to the team."

Jim Bunning uncorks the final pitch to clinch a perfect game.
(UPI/Corbis photo)

# NO ANYTHINGS: BUNNING A DOLLARS-AND-CENTS GUY

JUNE 22, 1964
BY STAN HOCHMAN

Jim Bunning pitches for a living. When you've got seven kids and they wear nice clothes, and you live in a rambling house in the suburbs, and you drive an air-conditioned car, it's got to be a good living.

Bunning pitched a perfect game, no hits, no runs, no anythings. Twenty-seven up and 27 down, while the Phillies battered the Mets 6-0 in the first game of a steamy doubleheader at Shea Stadium.

He does not expect a ticker-tape parade or a truckload of gifts or even a new contract from the Phillies. "I don't expect extra," Bunning said, blinking up at a cluster of writers. "It's part of the job. You get paid to pitch."

This was after an usher bustled up demanding a yes-or-no answer from "The Ed Sullivan Show." "For what?" Bunning asked, which is the equivalent of "How much?"

"When someone asks me to go on television, I ask how much," Bunning explained. He's 32 years old. He's a stockbroker in the winter, and he knows the value of a buck.

Maybe it sounded crass to talk about money at a time like that. Heck, it was the first regular-season perfect game since Charlie Robertson did it for the White Sox in 1922.

Bunning is a dollars-and-cents guy. It shows in the grim way he pitches, tumbling off the mound to get the maximum out of his sidearm delivery.

"Sure I talked about [the no-hitter]. I talked during the last one, too [For Detroit in 1958]. That way you're not disappointed. When I pitched that one-hitter in Houston, I talked, and after the guy got the hit, I didn't feel so bad.

"I'm a better pitcher now. I know how to pitch better. I threw a little harder then."

One run could have been enough, but the Phillies got six, and Bunning drove in two of them. "That was pretty good," Casey Stengel said after the muggy day was over.

"He finished strong and he deserves credit. He showed he was bearing down in a lot of ways. Like swing the bat, running 'em out. I knew he could pitch good, because he pitched for me in the All-Star Game."

The Mets fans are in a class by themselves, with their bedsheet banners and buglers and chanting. But by the eighth inning, they were behind Bunning, every goofy one of them.

The crowd screamed, and the Phillies came spilling out of the dugout to swarm all over Bunning. "I feel great," Bunning said, but it won't make a big difference in his life.

"I'll relax for a couple of days. Then I figure I'll pitch Saturday in St. Louis. We've got three games with the Cubs, then Dennis Bennett will probably open in St. Louis. Then I'll pitch again."

It sounded professional and it was. Jim Bunning pitches for a living.

Cincinnati speedster Chico Ruiz dazzles teammates with a daring
steal of home in the sixth inning with Frank Robinson at bat.
(Philadelphia Inquirer photo by Al Deans)

# PHILS PLAYED FOR RUN— REDS GOT IT

SEPTEMBER 21, 1964
BY STAN HOCHMAN

The other guys keep shuffling marked cards, but they deal themselves royal flushes, so what are you gonna do? The other guys keep rolling loaded dice, but they keep coming up seven, and that's a winner.

It came up seven again. Chico Ruiz stole home with Frank Robinson at bat in the sixth inning and the Reds beat the Phillies 1-0.

Art Mahaffey threw a strike to Robinson, while Ruiz was working up the courage to steal home. "On the first pitch he only looked at me once," Ruiz said. "He winds up slow. I thought, if he does it again, I'll go."

Mahaffey blissfully went into his windup, then saw Ruiz churning for the plate, and uncorked a wild pitch past Clay Dalrymple's desperate reach.

"I know Mahaffey was late reacting," said Robinson. "He rushed at the last second. I just have to protect the runner."

It is not a smart play, stealing home with Robinson up. Because Robinson is the only guy hitting over .300 in the Cincinnati lineup. Because Robinson gets $60,000 a year to drive in runs. Because Robinson has driven in more than 120 runs three of the last five seasons.

"I don't think it's a good play," acting manager Dick Sisler said afterwards. "That's the big hitter up there, the man getting all the money. I know I wouldn't call for it."

The loaded dice had come up seven again. The magic number stuck at seven, and the Reds moved to within 5 $\frac{1}{2}$ games of the Phillies with 11 left to play.

Gene Mauch didn't think too much of it either. "If Chico Ruiz attempts to steal home for me with Frank Robinson up," Mauch whispered hoarsely afterwards, "he sure as hell better be safe."

If Sisler thought it was a bad play, and Mauch thought it was a bad play, what was Ruiz thinking about? "I knew that was the best hitter up there," he said later, "so I was hoping I'd be safe. I didn't want to hear what the manager would say if I was out.

"I think I'll keep my record perfect. I don't think I'll try it again."

It wound up being the winning run because John Tsitouris shut the Phillies out on six hits. That makes seven one-run games in a row for the Phillies and two of the last three decided by a guy stealing home with only surprise and a swift pair of legs going for him.

And how did Robinson react to Ruiz' gambling gambol? "Surprised?" he said. "I just wasn't thinking about it. That's the first time that's happened while I was at bat. I think it surprised everybody."

Everybody was surprised, including Tsitouris, who pitched his first shutout of the season and brought his record to 8-11. "I didn't know what was happening," the stocky right-hander said. "Here he comes, with the best hitter up. I wondered what was going to happen next."

Rick Wise hit two homers in his no-hitter in 1971.
(Daily News photo by Elwood P. Smith)

# NOW RICK'S IMMORTAL, TOO

## JUNE 23, 1971
## BY BILL CONLIN

Rick Wise will never forget the afternoon he won his first big-league baseball game.

It was June 21, 1964, against the Mets, and Jim Bunning had just pitched his historic Father's Day perfect game.

It was the toughest encore for an 18-year-old rookie in baseball history.

"I didn't give up a hit until the fourth inning," Wise recalled after his two–home run no-hitter against the Reds, a 4-0 Phils win. "I couldn't figure out why the crowd let out this tremendous sarcastic cheer after the first hit. Then it struck me.

"It was the first base runner of the afternoon."

Bunning walked over to Wise's locker and pumped Rick's hand. "Thanks, fellow immortal," Rick said, smiling.

"Rick was great, but it was not his best stuff of the year," said catcher Tim McCarver. "He was more overpowering against San Francisco, New York and Houston. But anytime you no-hit these guys, you've accomplished a helluva feat.

"Pete Rose was the last guy in the world I wanted up there hitting with two outs in the ninth. I told him, 'Anybody else but you.' Nobody can say Rick didn't earn that last out. Pete was really grinding.

"When the ball left his bat, my heart jumped into my throat, but it went right at [third baseman John] Vukovich."

First baseman Deron Johnson listened to McCarver at the next locker. "First no-hitter, huh?" Deron asked. "I might be close to a record. This was the sixth I've played in. Jim Maloney had three of them, then Ken Johnson pitched one against the Reds for Houston and got beat 1-0. With the Phillies, I played in the one Bill Stoneman threw for Montreal, and now this one.

"They're all great. They really make you bear down, trying to make the plays that keep it going."

Pitching coach Ray Rippelmeyer reported Wise needed only 95 pitches to smother the Reds, who were no-hit by the Cubs' Ken Holtzman here less than three weeks ago.

"Rick threw 56 fastballs and 39 breaking balls," Rip said. "He made 19 pitches in the ninth inning, and 17 were fastballs, which shows you how he was mixing them up until the ninth."

Rick had a perfect game until walking short-stop Dave Concepcion with one out in the sixth, running the count to 3-0, throwing a strike, then losing him with a high pitch.

"Right there I think I was starting to tire briefly," Rick said. "Tim came out and told me to take a few deep breaths and relax. I took my inside shirt off between innings and I was a lot cooler after that."

Steve Carlton poses after his 20th win in 1972,
which extended his winning streak to 15 games.
(Daily News photo by Elwood P. Smith)

# JUST SUPER, STEVE!

AUGUST 17, 1972
BY BILL CONLIN

Blue Wednesday. Only 10,385 fans turned out on a lovely, cool evening to watch the Phillies perform an 8-2 floperoo for the Reds.

Blue Wednesday, Manager Paul Owens grumbled. Bad vibes all over the clubhouse.

The thing Steve Carlton does to his team is incredible. He walks to the mound and the Phillies become a snarling wolfpack of opportunists who score enough to win, make the right plays, hustle and display the machismo of a rising star in the National League firmament.

"His attitude when he's out there can get a lot of guys going," said catcher John Bateman after the Phillies pounded Ross Grimsley, Ed Sprague and Clay Carroll for 16 hits to keep Carlton's remarkable streak alive, 9-4. It was the 20th victory for The Franchise, his 15th straight. He joins Lefty Grove, Rube Marquard and Carl Hubbell as the fourth left-hander in history to win 15 or more in a row.

"Instead of looking for ways to lose, the way some guys on a losing club do, he looks for ways to win," Bateman said. "After giving up three runs in the third the way he did, a lot of guys would throw in the towel. That's when he said, 'Give me the ball and let's go.'"

It is his dogged refusal to recognize the possibility of defeat that infects the team when he pitches.

"Playing on a losing ball club is no guarantee you're going to lose," Carlton said after allowing four runs for the first time since he beat New York, 9-4, on June 29. "Each night is a new chance to win. What happened tonight is an indication of what it can be like here as soon as we have the enthusiasm on a continuous basis. The atmosphere tonight was tremendous."

The atmosphere is always tremendous when 46,635 fans show up at Veterans Stadium unannounced on a Thursday night to watch a superb solo artist do his thing.

"That's what it'll be like every game if we're fighting for a pennant," said shortstop Larry Bowa. "I was psyched. I felt like I was playing in a World Series."

"A game like this makes a difference," offered pitcher Dick Selma. "You get a knot in your stomach instead of your throat."

"He's been a lot better than he was tonight," said Manager Paul Owens. "In fairness, we haven't scored him a multitude of runs, but we've backed him up with some pretty good ball. What happened out here tonight is an indication of what we can expect if we can give this town a winner, and this man is going to be a big part of any success we have."

Mike Schmidt proudly holds up four bats representing
his four homers in a single game.
(UPI/Corbis photo)

# SCHMIDT NAILS 'EM

APRIL 17, 1976
BY BILL CONLIN

It wasn't the smartest thing Mike Schmidt ever did. It almost cost him some playing time and a place in baseball history.

Schmidt was shagging in left field and somebody remarked that he looked like he invented the position the way he was gliding under difficult wind-blown flies. But Mike is never as perfect as he thinks he should be. He misjudged a twisting fly and caught it with the middle finger of his throwing hand.

The nail was split almost to the cuticle, the first joint swollen and discolored.

"I think I can swing a bat," Schmidt said the next day, taping a foam rubber cushion on his 'gamer.' "I can hold that finger off a little. I just hope I can throw."

Holding his finger off the bat, Schmidt went 2-for-8 in Montreal, hurting physically, and mentally upset over a Rich Ashburn column suggesting he was overmatched in the No. 3 spot in Danny Ozark's batting order.

What happened in Chicago was almost beyond belief. Batting in the No. 6 spot, Schmidt became the first National Leaguer in this century to hit four consecutive homers. His fourth, a two-run shot to left-center in the 10th inning, gave the Phillies, down 12-1 and 13-2, a heroic 18-16 victory over the Cubs.

Schmidt made some mental and physical adjustments before the game.

"I had a long talk with Dick Allen before the game," Schmidt said, swathing his bat in sanitary socks for delivery to the Hall of Fame. "I can't say I was down in the mouth, but he's a good friend and I needed a little boost. He got my mind right."

The finger was still throbbing with pain when he made contact. Mike decided to use one of Tony Taylor's bats, a model an inch shorter and an ounce lighter but with a little more wood below the barrel.

"All the lighter bat did was keep me from opening my shoulder too soon," he said. "I was probably opening a little early to compensate for the finger."

Terry Harmon loaned him an ancient tee shirt, guaranteed to be "loaded with hits," the seldom-used utility infielder said.

All the forces—occult, physical, pyschological—converged at home plate for Schmidt.

Every pitcher who went to the mound leaned into a sirocco-hot southwest gale that froze the banners atop the scoreboard in center.

"When I first came to Wrigley Field they used to bleed me to death with breaking balls," Schmidt said. "I was pulling way around, trying to put the ball out of the park. Slowly but surely I realized I could hit 'em out just by using a normal, level swing. The longer I'm in this game, maybe I'll learn to adapt to certain parks, but right now I'll just settle for solid contact.

"Hell, I remember games here with the wind blowing in your face at 50 miles an hour rather than blowing out. You can hit your best shot and the ball keeps coming back at you."

It had to rank as one of the most explosive demonstrations in baseball history. The event was so overpowering, nobody seemed to notice that the manager didn't move from his dugout seat to congratulate Schmidt until after the fourth homer.

And the seven runs the Cubs scored in the second inning off a shot pitcher named Steve Carlton went as unnoticed as the first tentative snowflakes in a blizzard.

Mike Schmidt watches his second home run of the day leave the
ballpark. Schmidt's homer led the Phils to a 23-22 victory over the
Cubs in a slugfest that tied a major league home run record.
(AP/Wide World Photos)

# PHILS DO NUMBER ON CUBS

MAY 17, 1979
BY BILL CONLIN

Rawley Eastwick looked at Jim Lonborg. Jim Lonborg looked at Rawley Eastwick. Soon the warden and the priest would be coming for them.

They were the only inmates left on Death Row, and in the ninth inning it was Eastwick's turn to be fitted with a black hood and led before the Wrigley Field firing squad.

The crazies who sit beside the visitor's bullpen in the Cubs' cozy asylum rained gallows humor on the reliever while he lobbed his preliminary warm-ups.

There had already been a dizzying barrage of 44 runs and 49 hits, a great day for hitters even in a good slo-pitch softball league. The relentless cannonade had already included 10 homers, the Cubs had come storming back from the humiliation of a 21-9 deficit and now the scoreboard read, Cubs 22, Phillies 22.

Eastwick was next, and the 14,952 fans were ready to watch another one of Danny Ozark's Christians taking on their aroused lions.

"A fan yelled, 'Hey, Rawley, it's gonna be you and Bruce Sutter next, and you're gonna lose,'" Eastwick said after Mike Schmidt's 10th-inning homer gave the Phillies a record-toppling 23-22 victory. It's the only thing he heard yelled at him he could repeat.

The first inning alone produced a total of 13 runs and 14 hits, including four homers, a triple and a double.

All things are possible in Wrigley when the hot south wind hammering off the prairies starches the flag to attention atop this rococo remnant of a time when all major league baseball was played on green grass in God's own daylight. But this was ridiculous.

Yesterday it blew straight out at 2,030 miles an hour. And suddenly, baseball was a game played by hitters of gigantic stature in a phone booth.

"I knew we were in trouble when we scored seven runs in the first inning," said Larry Bowa, who collected five of the 24 Phillies' hits and scored four runs. "I saw the way the ball was flying around out there and said, 'No way seven is gonna be enough.'"

"When the conditions in this park are like they were today, the .220 hitter suddenly becomes the .300 hitter," Ron Reed said. "Everybody is swinging from his butt. Hell, even I felt like a hitter when I was up there. I was trying to pop one out."

While the mice roared, the genuine mashers like Dave Kingman and Schmidt stood at the plate looking as menacing as King Kong. The pitchers, conversely, had to feel like a troupe of Singers' Midgets wading through a swamp infested with alligators.

Schmidt's 14th homer, a cannon shot over the bleachers on a 3-2 Bruce Sutter pitch, didn't arouse feelings of overconfidence on the Phillies' bench.

"Was I comfortable with a one-run lead?" Ozark said. "Hell, no. We had already proved that a 12-run lead wasn't worth bleep."

Looking back at the smoking ruins of Wrigley Field, Danny Ozark said that the wind wasn't that much of a factor in his mind. That's like saying the printing press wasn't a factor in human development or that the invention of the wheel was overrated.

"I've seen it blow out like that here and shut-outs were pitched," Danny said. "But I've never seen a game anything like this. Hell, 50 hits! That's more than I used to get in a season."

19

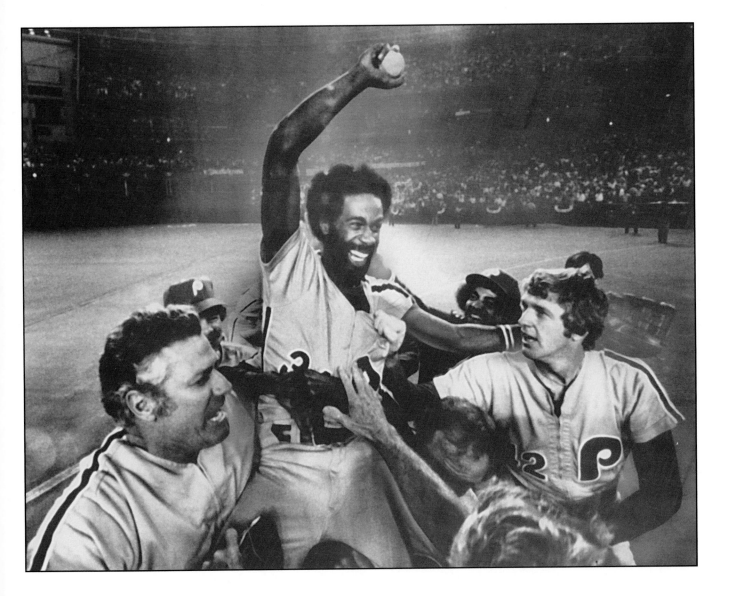

Garry Maddox is carried, hero-style, on the shoulders of his
teammates after catching the final out in Game 5 of the NLCS.
(Daily News photo by Denis O'Keefe)

# MADDOX TAKES RIDE
# OF HIS LIFE

OCTOBER 12, 1980
BY RAY DIDINGER

When they immortalize the Phillies' 1980 pennant clinching on canvas, when they chisel the whole crazy scene in stone or squeeze it onto a postage stamp, it will come down to Garry Maddox's victory ride. It will come down to Garry Maddox bouncing along on the shoulders of his teammates, his fists clenched above his head, the brilliant outline of his sideburns bristling against the bright Astrodome roof.

It was a game that decided perhaps the "greatest" postseason series in baseball history, a game that turned on one sudden flick of Garry Maddox' bat. With two outs in the 10th inning, Maddox stroked a Frank LaCorte fastball to center field. Terry Puhl charged the ball but couldn't come up with it. It skipped past him, Del Unser scored the decisive run and Maddox streaked into second base like a cheetah sniffing a fresh kill.

Then in the bottom of the 10th, the final two Houston Astro batters hit fly balls to Maddox. He watched them both disappear into his Gold Glove, and then in an uncharacteristic display of emotion, Garry Maddox danced with joy over the 8-7 victory.

He rushed toward the infield, toward the mob of Phillies who had come streaming from the dugout. He leaped into the arms of Larry Bowa, then into the arms of Manager Dallas Green. "I've never had a feeling like it," Maddox said. "This was such an emotional series there were so many turns, so many comebacks. You just ached on every pitch.

"I can't say enough about this team. These guys

never quit. They never let down. When Houston came back to tie us [in the eighth], the guys on the bench encouraged us, told us to get our heads up. I got the winning hit," Maddox said, "but I'll tell you, this was a real team effort. We got great clutch hitting, we got some great defensive plays, and Dick [Ruthven] did a superior job in relief.

"When we got to the playoffs, we dedicated ourselves to one thing, and that was going all the way. We knew we wouldn't be satisfied—and our fans wouldn't be satisfied—by anything less than a National League pennant."

Coach Bobby Wine edged through the group of newsmen around Maddox and he embraced the center fielder. "Great job," Wine said.

"Thank you," Maddox said. His voice was weak, filling with emotion. "I've never felt this way before . . . never in my life," Maddox said. "I'm elated but I'm almost limp. I'm tired from playing. I'm exhausted from jumping up and down in the dugout yelling.

"I'm elated. All the disappointment, all the frustrations I felt in years gone by are washed away. Hey, I can't tell you how it felt to have those guys pick me up and carry me off that field. I didn't know they were gonna do that. In fact, I didn't know what they were doing at first. When I realized it, I thought, 'This must be a dream. This all has to be a dream.'"

So a season of conflicting emotion, a season tinted with controversy—perhaps real, perhaps imagined—ended happily for Garry Lee Maddox. The memory, like the bottle he sipped from, had no jagged edges.

Phillies closer Tug McGraw jumps from the mound after he struck out Royals' Willie Wilson for the final out of the 1980 World Series. (Daily News photo by E.W. Faircloth)

# POP THE CORKS!

OCTOBER 21, 1980
BY BILL CONLIN

Bob Boone gloved the last fastball Tug McGraw had left in his weary arm and the Phillies waded joyously onto the East bank of the River Jordan.

The final scene of the 1980 World Series looked like something Cecil B. DeMille would have filmed in the Promised Land the Phillies finally reached last night with a 4-1 victory. They erupted joyously into each other's arms, surrounded by new centurions on horseback, helmeted soldiery carrying truncheons, snarling attack dogs and a whooping cast of 65,838 extras aflame with passion, eyes blazing with the Phils' first World Series title.

The Game 6 script was dramatically correct. Steve Carlton, the Sphinx of the Schuylkill, paralyzed the Kansas City Royals for seven wonderful innings while leading man Mike Schmidt and Company carved him a 4-0 lead. When Carlton put the first two Royals on base in the eighth, Dallas Green, heeding a "Lefty's had it" signal from Boone, brought in Tug McGraw to part the rally-tossed waters of the Red Sea one more time.

This time Tug McGraw was out of miracles. His tank was empty; his cup ranneth under. He knew warming up that if he did it again it would be with mirrors, with memory, with whatever little extra he could reach back for and somehow find. He survived a bases-loaded crucible in the eighth, allowing only one run.

So there was McGraw in the ninth, the bases loaded and only one out. There were suddenly 658,380 white knuckles in the Vet, 658,375 if you count Phillies special assignment scout Hugh Alexander, who helped orchestrate the plan for keeping sprinters Willie Wilson, U.L. Washington and Frank White off base. "Ah was thinkin' don't that kid make me look bad now," Alexander drawled. "Ah could see Tug didn't have that good live stuff."

White hit a foul that came down in front of the Phillies dugout. Boone has the surest hands in the catching fraternity and he hasn't dropped one in years. You could trust him to catch an infant dropped from the 10th story of a burning building. But he dropped this one. In one of the most remarkable reflex plays in history, Pete Rose gloved it before it hit the track or was snapped up by a German shepherd. He looked like Samu the Killer Whale surfacing to snap up a thrown herring. "It didn't surprise me that Pete did it," McGraw said. "He's always there when you need him."

McGraw still had Wilson to deal with, a 230-hit collector during the regular American League season, who in this tournament resembled a windmill jousting with Don Quixote. Wilson had already tied

23

Steve Carlton pitched seven strong innings
during decisive Game 6 of the World Series.
(Daily News photo by Norman Y. Lono)

the Series record for most strikeouts when Carlton blew him away in the first and third innings.

McGraw knew he had a pressing, confused fish on the end of the line. The question was, as the count went to 1-2, did he have the strength to reel him in?

"I was saying to myself, 'I really have a chance to be a dog out here,'" Tug said. "I was out of gas on the mound for the first time this season. I had visions of Wilson getting a hit and them sinking the tugboat they named after me yesterday. Or maybe they would have renamed it, 'Tug McGraw Sinker.' Rather than get myself hyper about it, I decided to use it as a motivating tool. I got myself up to throw one, last, good fastball."

It did not challenge Nolan Ryan's 103 mph record. But it blew by Wilson's late swing, and McGraw, like F. Scott Fitzgerald's gold-hatted, high-dancing lover, gave one final, triumphal leap. "I don't know what Dallas had in mind," he said, "but if I didn't get Wilson I was calling him to the mound because I had nothing left. Nothing."

When Carlton had completed his pregame warm-ups to Keith Moreland, he flashed a thumbs-up sign like a World War II bomber pilot taking off for a milk run over an undefended target. In the first inning, he had the kind of stuff that put the press box on no-hitter alert so many times during the regular season. He was overpowering and the slider was there. But in the second inning the Royals went into their four-corners stall. Amos Otis was stepping in and stepping out, pawing in the dirt, resining his bat handle. Carlton walked him. Willie Mays Aikens did the same number and also wound up looking at ball four.

In the fifth, Carlton struck them both out. "Lefty went after those guys to embarrass them, I know that," said Green. "I know he was trying for a strikeout every time and he got a couple of 'em."

The offense broke through for Carlton in the third against towering right-hander Rich Gale, whose selection over experienced left-hander Paul Splittorff will be second-guessed in Kansas City as long as there are prairies.

Boone led it off with a walk. Pete Rose gave the vast national TV audience an at-bat that had to have people who know and love the shades and nuances of inside baseball in ecstasy, faking the bunt, faking the bunt again, swinging away, faking the bunt and finally dropping a 3-1 pitch toward third that had George Brett backpedaling toward the bag. Rose legged it out and the bases were loaded with nobody out. Mike Schmidt lashed a line single to right-center. Boone scored. Lonnie "Tumbleweed" Smith scored despite falling down after rounding third and the Phillies led, 2-0.

They roared when Smith legged a single to center into a double leading off the fifth and exploded when he scored on Bake McBride's slow chopper to short after motoring to third on Rose's fly to center.

They roared with the frenzy of a Roman Coliseum mob in the sixth when Bowa doubled to left batting right-handed against reliever Splittorff, Wilson playing him so wrong that National League scouts must have been chuckling. The shortstop, who had a grinding, emotional, born-again Series, scooted home when Boone lined a single to center.

It was 4-0. And the way Carlton was burying the Royals, it was as good as history.

But nothing has come easily to this fascinating collection of athletes this season.

Carlton's last powerful inning was the sixth, which he ended with his seventh strikeout. "He was starting to feather his fastball," Green said. "But until the end his fastball was there tonight." So Green handed the ball to the reliever they named a tugboat after. Dallas had to believe Tug could do it one more time after doing it so many times in the most exhausting October of his career.

With horses pawing the turf, attack dogs baring their fangs, riot police ringing the box seats, with 65,838 people screaming for him to close it out, Tug reached back for all he had left to give.

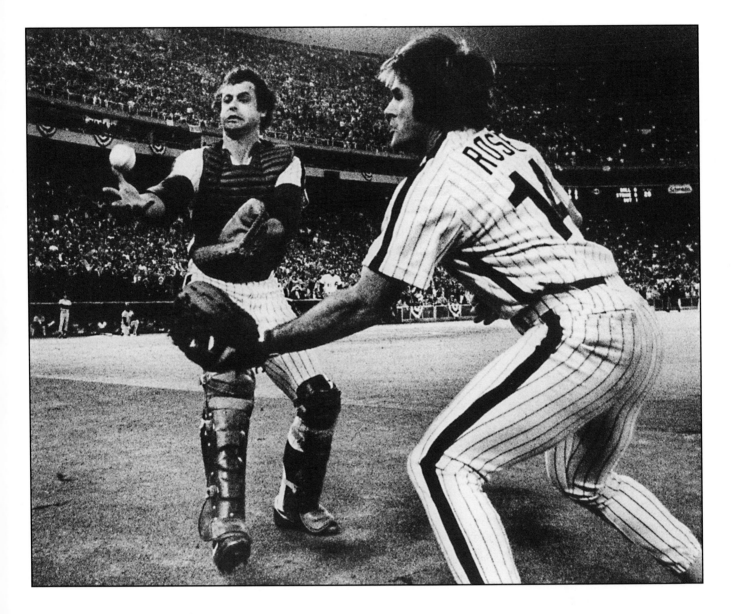

The ball pops out of catcher Bob Boone's mitt but Pete Rose is
there to recover. (Daily News photo by Norman Y. Lono)

# ROSE WAS JOHNNY ON THE SPOT

OCTOBER 21, 1980
BY PHIL JASNER

Later this week, after you've thoroughly discussed this World Series championship, after you've read the papers, scanned the TV replays, savored the parade and put your thoughts in some semblance of perspective, ask yourself this:

Isn't this the reason the Phillies got Pete Rose in the first place?

"You'll have to ask Ruly [club president Ruly Carpenter] that," Pete said in the clubhouse early this morning, after his team had won, 4-1, ending a frantic six-game scramble with Kansas City.

"If he got me just for this, though, I wouldn't have had to play till today, would I?"

He was a gem in an acre of diamonds, getting three hits, bunting successfully to load the bases in the two-run third, making a remarkable acrobatic save on Frank White's ninth-inning foul pop that tumbled off catcher Bob Boone's glove.

"When it was hit," Pete said, "it could've been either of us making the play. I couldn't hear him, but I happened to see him make the call.

"Normally, it's his ball, and with a man at third, I'd be the cutoff man to home. But with all the cameras over there near the dugout . . . all the equipment and stuff, I thought there was a chance he might trip or something. I stayed there, I normally don't do that.

"He's so good on pop-ups . . . It wasn't a mistake, though, it was a tough play.

"This team seemed to really learn a lot the last two months. We learned how to play together, how to approach a big game, how to attack a big series. We never did it the easy way, either. We had to be backed into a corner first."

Maybe the Phillies, before last night, didn't know about World Series championships, but being backed into corners, that they knew about.

"These guys have been so close so many times." Rose said, "it probably means even more to them to win now. The fans? All they wanted us to do is what we accomplished."

But isn't Pete Rose the one who told us he's not a good World Series hitter because he doesn't know the pitchers?

"And if you analyze what I did in this one," he replied, "you'll see I got no hits the first game, no hits the second, one in the third, then finished strong because I had seen those guys throw. If the World Series was 51 out of 100, I could get a lot of hits. But it's still four out of seven.

"This, though . . . this is the first trip through this little bed of roses for these guys. Too bad it's a year late, but we just couldn't overcome what we had to go through. We had 23 guys on the disabled list, six broken bones.

"This team is different . . . it's even a different team than it was in April, May and June. They attack big series now, they have the kind of feeling that, even if we're down, 8-0, we think we can come back and win.

"Pressure? I'm a firm believer that all the pressure is in the playoffs, that there's no pressure in the World Series. But here, with this team, the pressure can build up, and people don't want to hear all the bullbleep. These fans came in raring to go . . . they were after something they had never had.

"We've got Mike Schmidt the MVP, Steve Carlton the Cy Young winner, Tug McGraw the best bullpen pitcher," he said. "Maybe this isn't the '61 Yankees or the '76 Reds, but it's the best club we've had. Somebody asked me if winning a third Series makes it old hat. Old hat? Coming to a new city doing this, how could anybody think that?"

Stan Musial laughs on the night Pete Rose broke his
record for most hits in National League history.
(Daily News photo by E.W. Faircloth)

# ROSE JUST KEEPS ON TICKING

AUGUST 10, 1981
BY STAN HOCHMAN

There are no calendars in the playgrounds of Pete Rose's mind. Only tumult, action, excitement, a hard-way four to be rolled with the dice, a "15" to be hit when the dealer's got a 10 showing.

He is 40 years bold, not 40 years old. And nobody in the whole cockeyed history of the National League has gotten more hits. He passed Stan Musial. Fourth time up. Switched to a lighter bat. Hit a Mark Littell fastball. Lashed a bouncing single into left field for his 3,631st hit.

And afterward, they pestered him with questions about Ty Cobb, who had 4,191 hits. It is a media sickness, the afternoon paper angle, the overnighter, the sidebar swarm. It shamelessly steals the joy from the moment. If there had been a reporter at the peak of Everest, would he have asked Sir Edmund Hillary, "What about Kilimanjaro?" Pete Rose answered patiently, earthly, honestly. The way he always does.

"You're asking me questions only The Man Upstairs knows the answers to," he said. "I can't answer them.

"I knew I was gonna break the record," he said. "Now, I've got three things on my mind. A world championship. Leading the league in hits. Winning the batting title . . .

"You might think I'm an egomaniac. But I've got things that keep me pushing. If you're a good player and you've got pride, it's inside you to play good. People ask about incentives in a split season. Hey, I've got the incentive to lead the league.

"Me and Stan Musial, we've led the league in hits seven times. Nobody's ever done it eight. That kind of stuff keeps me going."

Musial was there, alongside Rose, on a podium, behind a clutter of microphones. Musial had 725 doubles. Rose has 666. That's a target. That's a number he can challenge. That's one he can talk about without someone getting maudlin and suggesting it is out of reach for a 40-year-old.

Rose cannot change. Why should he? Why would anyone want him to? Muhammad Ali once said, "I don't have to be what you want me to be." And Rose is that way too.

And when he slipped the metal doughnut-shaped weight off the bat following his practice waggles, he handed it to his son, Petey.

"I usually throw the ring to the batboy," Rose said. "But this time I handed it to Petey. He was down a little. Third time up, he said, 'If you don't get it tonight, you'll get it tomorrow.'"

"I said to him, 'Watch this time . . . I'm gonna get the hit.' I was just trying to pick him up. He worries sometimes. He's just a little boy.

"Littell started me off with a slider for a strike. The only breaking ball I saw all night. And then he came back with a fastball, inside, and I knew it was going through when I hit it."

He got to first base, took that aggressive turn and then clapped his hands as he returned to the bag. The crowd erupted. First-base coach Ruben Amaro embraced Rose, and then little Petey was there, leading the dugout swarm, as 3,631 balloons drifted into the summer sky, vibrating with cheers.

"You know the reaction of the fans," he said. "They're gonna stand up and cheer. But you don't know they're gonna stand up and cheer that long.

"Petey was the first one out there, and I was surprised at that. He said, 'Nice going, Pop.' And I gave him the ball. So it worked out nice."

Pete Rose high-fives his son, Petey, after
breaking Stan Musial's NL record for hits.
(Daily News photo by E.W. Faircloth)

# NEW HOT LINE: REAGAN TO ROSE

## AUGUST 10, 1981
### BY STAN HOCHMAN

He'd gotten a handshake from the commissioner and kind words from the general manager and the club owner, and now he was splattering words off the griddle of excitement, like little sizzles of cooking oil. The red phone rang.

"Tell the president to wait a minute," Pete Rose said.

It was the president calling, but first a voice said, "One moment, please."

The moment stretched into an awkward 50 seconds, and Rose tried to fill the time with patter. "Maybe the operators have gone on strike?" he said. And as the pause grew longer, he said, "Good thing there isn't a missile on the way."

The red phone would ring three more times before Ronald Reagan was there, ready to congratulate Rose for setting a National League record for career hits—3,631.

"I'll tell you," Reagan said, "I've had so much trouble getting this line. I think I had to wait longer than you did to break the record."

"We were gonna give you five more minutes and then that was it," Rose said, while the media mob chuckled.

"I just wanted to call and congratulate you," Reagan said. "I know how you must feel and I think it's great."

"Well, thank you very much," Rose said. "I know you're a baseball fan and we appreciate your taking time out to call us here in Philadelphia. I know all the fans appreciate it and Pete Rose and Pete Rose the second appreciate it too."

"I can tell you that you are right about being a fan," Reagan said. "And as a matter of fact, I was a sports announcer, broadcasting major league baseball, before I ever had any kind of a job like I have now. But this is really a thrill, and I know how everyone must feel about it after the long dry spell waiting for the season to get under way, and you've really brought it in style."

"Well, thank you very much," Rose said. "You play a good football player too."

There was the awkward dialogue of good-bye, and that was it. Pete Rose, the kid from Bold Face Park in Cincinnati, chatting with The Gipper, like two guys in a tavern on River Road. Had Rose been too flip, too chummy?

"I learned a long time ago," he said later, "to be yourself. I was respectful, but I was just myself. I talked to Mr. George Bush [the vice president] yesterday in Cleveland, Mr. Jimmy Carter had me down to Washington twice.

"They had a luncheon for me in Washington. I was telling jokes. Saying 'bleep' and 'huh' and everything. Had a four-star general and a five-star general and all them secretaries of education and welfare sitting around and I was being myself.

"Look, I appreciate the president taking time out to call. I know how busy he is. How tough his job is."

He is Pete Rose, thorns and all. And he must be himself, even on special nights, talking to special people.

Mitch Williams jumps for joy as the Phillies clinch
the NLCS. (Daily News photo by George Reynolds)

# PHILLIES SHOW THE WORLD

OCTOBER 13, 1993
BY PAUL HAGEN

And then the night sky exploded with a thousand points of light that would capture the moment for posterity. Streamers floated from the upper reaches of a massive stadium literally rocked by sound. A lone helicopter buzzed overhead. Seconds later, police motorcycles, blue lights flashing, streamed onto the playing surface, accompanied by the mounted brigade that woke the echoes of the 1980 championship season.

It was 1:17 p.m. on Oct. 13, 1993, at the corner of Broad Street and Pattison Avenue in Philadelphia, Pennsylvania. Pinch hitter Bill Pecota struck out. A strange and wonderful odyssey had ended.

The Phillies are going to the World Series.

Against all odds, against all reason, against the team many considered the best in baseball, the Phillies wrestled the National League pennant from the two-time-champion Atlanta Braves with a 6-3 victory at Veterans Stadium.

That gave the Phillies the series, four games to two, and their first trip to the World Series since 1983.

"Sometimes you can't control what's meant to be, and this has been meant to be since spring training," center fielder Lenny Dykstra said. "It's hard to explain. Granted, Atlanta might be better position by position. They might be better pitcher by pitcher. Everybody thought we were done when we were blown out two straight games (14-3 and 9-4), but this was meant to be."

"On paper. Maybe we weren't the best team," said Larry Andersen, "but we had guts and grit. And now we're the National League champions and there's nothing like it. I'm just numb. It's like the ugly stepsister being invited to the ball by the best-looking guy in the class."

Added first baseman John Kruk, champagne dripping from his hair: "Call it luck, I don't know. Whatever it is, we're taking it. People may be surprised to find out that we won. Maybe when we wake up, we will be, too. All I know is that I'm wearing a hat and a shirt that say we're the National League champions and that's good enough for me."

Nobody, perhaps, could savor the moment more than catcher Darren Daulton. After the final out, Daulton jumped as if 10,000 volts had surged through his face mask.

"I've never had a better moment in baseball," he said later. "I went crazy out there. I've just never had that kind of emotion before. I saw the house rocking, to know that something has happened that meant so much to three or four million people . . . it's hard to explain."

Once again on a magic night, the don't-show-up-in-the-box-score nuances on which a game can hinge came up wearing candy-red pinstripes.

And then it was over and the scoreboard exploded into flashing variations of a theme—WE WIN and PHILS WIN and PHILLIES 1993 NATIONAL LEAGUE CHAMPIONS—in a scene that would have been hard for most people to envision.

Richie Ashburn and Mike Schmidt at their induction into the
Baseball Hall of Fame. (Daily News photo by G. W. Miller III)

# SCHMIDT, ASHBURN WOW 'EM

JULY 30, 1995
BY TED SILARY

Along with fellow ex-Phillie Rich Ashburn, it was Mike Schmidt's turn to be inducted into the Baseball Hall of Fame. Under beautiful skies in sweltering heat, it could not have gone better.

Schmidt, who wore a light-green suit for the occasion, received only love, adulation and, most important of all, courtesy from a crowd estimated by Hall officials at 25,000 to 28,000; no previous crowd had topped 20,000.

When Schmidt was asked in his post-induction press conference whether he expected 100 percent approval, he responded with an unqualified "No."

Schmidt mentioned that he had sought advice from Reggie Jackson and Mayor Ed Rendell. Before the ceremony, Rendell said there was "not a chance" that Phillie fans would wreck the occasion. And right he was.

Rendell laughed, "Know what the context was? Steve Carlton was with us. We were commiserating with each other, talking about how all three of us had the misfortune of talking to *Philadelphia* magazine."

Ah, *Philadelphia* magazine. In the July issue, Schmidt was quoted as saying: "It's hard for me to be positive, to have real good things to say about a town that never did anything for me. And, in general, made life miserable for me." Schmidt later apologized. Yesterday, after thanking almost everyone who aided his career, he paused, drew a breath and said, "And what about the Philly fans?" Oh boy, everybody thought. Here we go. Direction unknown.

Schmidt first said he is asked everywhere he goes what it was like to play in Philadelphia. Then he said, "Let me say this and make it short and as sweet as I possibly can. If I had to do it all over again, I'd do it in Philly. The only thing I'd change would be me. I'd be less sensitive. I would be more outgoing. I would be more appreciative of what you expected of me. My relationship with the Philadelphia fans has always been misunderstood. Can we put that to rest here today?"

While the fans applauded, Schmidt added, "I and my family sure hope we can.

"It's great that we see eye-to-eye on something isn't it, Philadelphia."

Ashburn, who wore a cream-colored sport coat, tan slacks and—surprise, surprise—removed his hat, was mostly funny and footloose during his remarks, at one juncture lamenting that he could not provide the multitudes with Tastykakes and pretzels, Schmidt was mostly serious.

Ashburn got emotional twice. In the middle of saying, "Ideally for me, this could have happened earlier because my father passed away," he heaved and began to cry. "Hang on," he added, trying to gather himself. "My twin sister passed away and we had a daughter, Jan, who died in a car accident in April 1987." Again he struggled. Then he looked at the positive. "On the other hand," he said, "our grandchildren are here. They wouldn't have been here 20 years ago. I was a little shaky about joining this select group. But they have been nice to all of us, and I appreciate it."

"In your professional life, in your whole life, it's hard to top a day like this," said Schmidt.

Boxing promoter Don King holds up Mike Tyson's
arm after he beat Buster Mathis at the Spectrum.
(Daily News photo by George Reynolds)

# A
# CENTURY OF
# BOXING

BY BERNARD FERNANDEZ

The last, best hope for Philadelphia to re-establish itself as a major boxing site probably came and went in December 1995, when a combination of factors brought former heavyweight champion Mike Tyson, the sport's most electrifying draw, to town on short notice for a bout with Buster Mathis Jr. at the CoreStates (now First Union) Spectrum.

Tyson's presence meant a national television audience on Fox would be tuned in, the sort of huge spotlight that hadn't been focused on America's self-proclaimed capital of boxing since regularly scheduled cards at the Spectrum ended in 1980. It was a chance for Philly to live up to its pugnacious, pugilistic reputation.

"I don't even know how I got here in the first place," Tyson said after finishing a workout in the Joe Hand Boxing Gym in Fishtown, the fight having been rejected in Atlantic City because of promoter Don King's federal indictment on wire-fraud charges.

"But I don't believe there is any such thing as coincidence. There's always a reason for something. We all know the history of those legendary Philadelphia fighters. I'm just happy to be here and be a part of it. I can be an extension of that history."

In truth, he might have written the final chapter of the big book on boxing in a city that once ate up megafights more hungrily than its beloved cheese steaks. A rusty Tyson stopped Mathis in three rounds in front of a heavily papered crowd estimated at between 8,000 and 10,000, although final attendance figures, paid or otherwise, never were revealed. There was considerable speculation that many overpriced tickets had been given away or severely discounted and that the promotion was awash in red ink.

Another bid to jump-start Philadelphia as a prime boxing destination, and not just the place of origination for standout fighters, also ended badly. North Philly's David Reid, the only U.S. gold medalist in boxing at the 1996 Atlanta Olympics, stopped former world champion Simon Brown in four rounds in his much-hyped professional homecoming, but paid attendance in the Apollo of Temple fell far below projections.

Goodbye, big dreams for recaptured glory. Hello, more comparatively low-budget fare at the 1,200-seat Blue Horizon, which is a great place to see a fight but is a far cry from the days when major

Joe Frazier sends Yemel Yanov, of Russia, to the canvas in a semifinal
heavyweight bout at the 1964 Olympics. A referee halted the bout and
gave Frazier the win. (AP/Wide World Photos)

events in the city regularly drew crowds from 30,000 to 130,000.

"The Mike Tyson fight probably could have done bonanza business if they had the intelligence to scale the tickets properly, but they overpriced the show and that killed it. I don't care how close it was to Christmas, I don't care how short the notice was, they had a chance to do something really special and they killed it," says J Russell Peltz, who has promoted boxing in Philadelphia since 1969, but was not involved in the Tyson-Mathis bout.

Boxing here is hanging on by its fingernails, as is the case in most major American cities that do not have casino gambling.

"Philadelphia is still one of the leading cities, if not the leading city, in producing boxing talent," says George Bochetto, Philadelphia boxing commissioner.

According to *The Ring*, the Philadelphia area had 14 fight clubs in operation by 1900 and was recognized as the leading city for purse money for non-championship bouts. Nearly every top fighter fought here, and legendary heavyweight Jack Johnson made more appearances in Philadelphia than in any other city except for his hometown of Galveston, Texas. That might be attributable in part to the city's reputation for being the most "open" in the country to black boxers.

With so many venues available, it really is no surprise that, over six decades of almost unchecked growth, Philadelphia gave the world such homegrown or adopted standouts as Philadelphia Jack O'Brien, Battling Levinsky, Benny Bass, Lew Tendler, Midget Wolgast, Bob Montgomery, Tommy Loughran, Al Ettore, Johnny Jadick, Harold Johnson, Wesley Mouson, Percy Bassett, George Benton, Joey Giardello and Joe Frazier.

"Boxing changed because the times changed," Peltz says. "Until oh, 1960, baseball and boxing were vying for the biggest pieces of the sports entertainment dollar. The NFL and NBA weren't nearly as big then as they are now. Hockey certainly wasn't. If you had a really big fight, you'd get a huge crowd outdoors in a stadium. It's not like that now, and hasn't been for a long time."

Not that Philly is alone in its benign neglect of boxing.

"New York probably can compete with the casino venues, but the people who can make it happen don't have the foresight," Peltz says. "You can't tell me that I can sell out the Blue Horizon on a consistent basis, but they can't put a first-class boxing program into the [5,000-seat] Theater at Madison Square Garden and sell it out every month."

Peltz believes boxing in Philadelphia can be brought back, if not all the way, then to something more substantial than what presently exists.

"Maybe a homegrown puncher who stays at home, who is developed at home, could do it," Peltz says.

"I'm not sure how far the Allen twins [Tiger and Rock, both of whom recently were crowned Pennsylvania Golden Gloves champions] can go, but the better they are, the less likely it is that they'll spend much of their careers in Philadelphia," says Nigel Collins, editor of *The Ring*. "If they're as good as David Reid and win Olympic gold medals, they'll start out with some high-powered promotional outfit and go where the money is."

That place, increasingly, is out of town.

---

| | | |
|---|---|---|
| Former Olympic gold medalist Joe Frazier, already recognized as heavyweight champion in six states and seven countries, captured the undisputed crown when WBA titlist Jimmy Ellis failed to answer the bell for the fifth round of their Feb. 16, 1970, bout at Madison Square Garden. | The rubber match of the Muhammad Ali-Joe Frazier trilogy, Oct. 1, 1975, proved to be the best. Frazier battered Ali for the better part of 10 rounds. But the champion, who had slumped on his stool between rounds until then, answered with perhaps the greatest four rounds of his career, landing continually to the head of Frazier, who could not answer the bell for the 15th round. Ali nearly fainted in his corner, but he remained champ. | The U.S. boxing team made a bold statement at the 1984 Olympics, as super heavyweight Tyrell Biggs and featherweight Meldrick Taylor each scored a decision to earn two of the USA's nine fistic gold medals. |

Jack Dempsey (facing camera) during a 1926 title bout he lost to Gene
Tunney at Sesqui Stadium, which eventually became known as JFK
Stadium. (Photo from The Philadelphia Inquirer collection)

# DEMPSEY A SHELL

SEPTEMBER 23, 1926
BY T. VON ZIEKURSCH

There was one good fighter in the ring at the Sesqui Stadium last night. He isn't the champion of the world today. He could have licked either of the men who fought for the heavyweight crown. His name is Tommy Loughran.

But he was only a side-show attraction, one of those put on to keep the interest of the 130,000 who had come to see Gene Tunney take the title away from Jack Dempsey.

Tunney is the ninth in succession to rule on the throne of the world's champions. He took the crown and scepter away from a sorry relic of a once-great fighter. He beat Dempsey to a decision. There couldn't have been one to question it when the judges, Frank Brown of Pittsburgh and Mike Bernstein of Wilkes-Barre, gave their verdict that Dempsey had been beaten and a new champion was to be named.

The critics were wrong. The experts erred. Honest confession may be a redeeming feature. If it is, we take advantage of it. We were wrong. Tunney fought as we had expected, as everyone had expected. Dempsey didn't.

Twice during those 10 long rounds Tunney took the lead. The rest of the time he fought a purely defensive fight, backing away, tying Dempsey up at close quarters, pecking away with his right at every opportunity.

If any one thing stood out in this fight, it was the fighting spirit of Dempsey, but spirit alone couldn't carry him to victory.

Tunney's camp had been nervous at the outset. By the fourth round the nervousness passed. They looked scornfully at Dempsey's corner.

They sent Tunney out with orders to fight for it. They were like dogs who sensed that time had come for the kill. But Tunney went out and fought as he has always fought, as he always will fight, waiting for the opening, a defensive fighter. He fought well. He was an expert swordsman winning from an old barbarian with a club.

Tunney's sun rose as Dempsey's set. Those who looked on wondered that they had picked Dempsey. It was only his shell in the ring last night. And the shell of brawn was beaten by brains, by a carefully planned fight, mapped out and carried out by a man who knew more than all the critics and all the experts, by the only man in the world who was really confident of the outcome, by the highest type of man who has ever held the heavyweight championship of the world—Gene Tunney, ex-Marine.

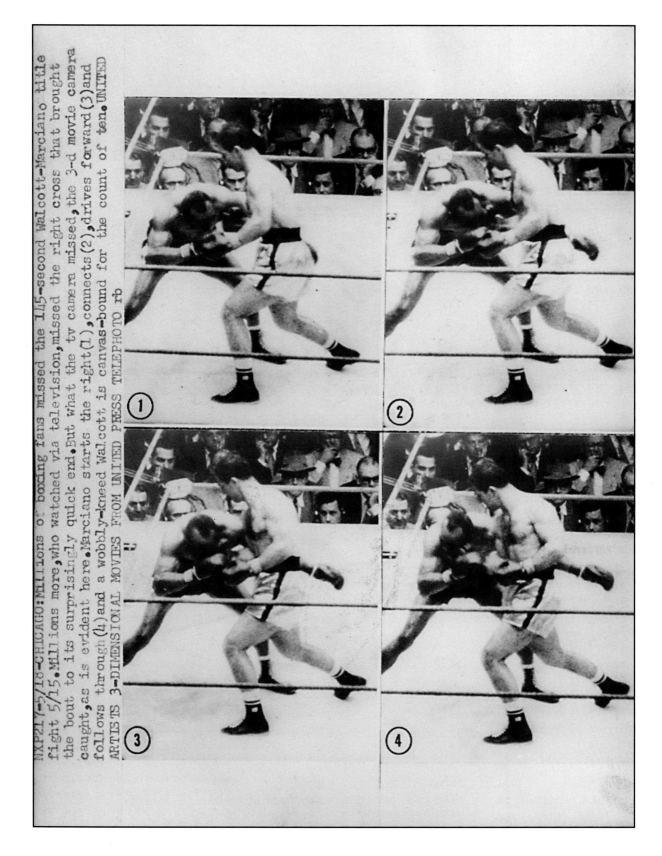

NXP21(-5/18-CHICAGO:Millions of boxing fans missed the 145-second Walcott-Marciano title fight 5/15.Millions more,who watched via television,missed the right cross that brought the bout to its surprisingly quick end.But what the tv camera missed,the 3-d movie camera caught,as is evident here.Marciano starts the right(1),connects(2),drives forward(3)and follows through(4)and a wobbly-kneed Walcott is canvas-bound for the count of ten.UNITED ARTISTS 3-DIMENSIONAL MOVIES FROM UNITED PRESS TELEPHOTO rb

Rocky Marciano retained his heavyweight boxing title by knock-
ing out Jersey Joe Walcott at 2:25 of the first round at Chicago
Stadium in a 1953 rematch of their 1952 bout in Philadelphia.
(UPI/Corbis photo)

# GREATEST FIGHT EVER WAGED IN BOWL

SEPTEMBER 23, 1952
BY LANSE MCCURLEY

There may be some who will tell you it was a lucky punch that smashed Joe Walcott into complete unconsciousness in the ring at the Municipal Stadium last night when the gods turned their favor on a new son of fame and fortune, and the championship of the world passed on to Rocky Marciano, but courage is never lucky, and youth is never chance, and the two of them powered one of the hardest blows ever thrown in the prize ring to turn the tide from its running up the sands of defeat and the shores of disappointment back to the deep glory of triumph.

It was a right hand that did the job, although Marciano followed in sequence with a left that tapped the falling champion on his way down, a low right that came from the side, with a round curve, a short slider curve to borrow an expression from the pitching mound, and it wasn't aimed except by heart, a great heart, a heart that wouldn't bruise into dismay or stop pulsing with hope under slash and cut, smash and jar, a heart that aimed in the general direction of a foe whose form was hazy through the blood that cascaded down over the eyes, and which denied the exhaustion that weighed limb, arm and leg.

No—you can't call such a punch luck because it was not sired by chance nor did it land by hazard—it was born of courage, the sort that makes immortal men who fight on to the death long after their weapons are apparently without ammunition, and their cause without hope, and they can no longer see or maneuver or do ought else but keep fighting, throwing punches, pressing triggers, knowing not defeat, ever, no matter how far off into the fog any whisper of victory may have dimmed.

So ended the greatest fight ever waged in our city bowl. On a high note. On a peak. With a dramatic suddenness that stunned the crowd as well as the fallen brown figure who was the victim. On a note of tragedy as poignant as any for Marciano as he floundered around, almost knocked out himself in the 11th round, down in the first, cut and beaten and back in the scoring, in the end as fickle as any siren held up to man as a warning. Betraying the one it was so wantonly smiling upon, Joe Walcott. And weirdly enough in the 13th round, a number unlucky through the ages, before a crowd of 40,379 people who paid $504,645, the second largest gate in the boxing history of this city.

So it ended with both of these modern gladiators covered with their own blood, Walcott's white trunks a red mess, Marciano bleeding from a cut on top of his skull, the champion, as if by some magic whose key is found by a few, growing spryer just at the time he should have been tottering from weakness, and the kid, the youngest, the epitome of strength, showing those signs of exhaustion which rightfully were the toll of his older opponent.

Strange, it was, dramatic, and tragic, but never let anyone tell you courage is luck and youth is chance and that Marciano did not win a great fight and beat a great fighter.

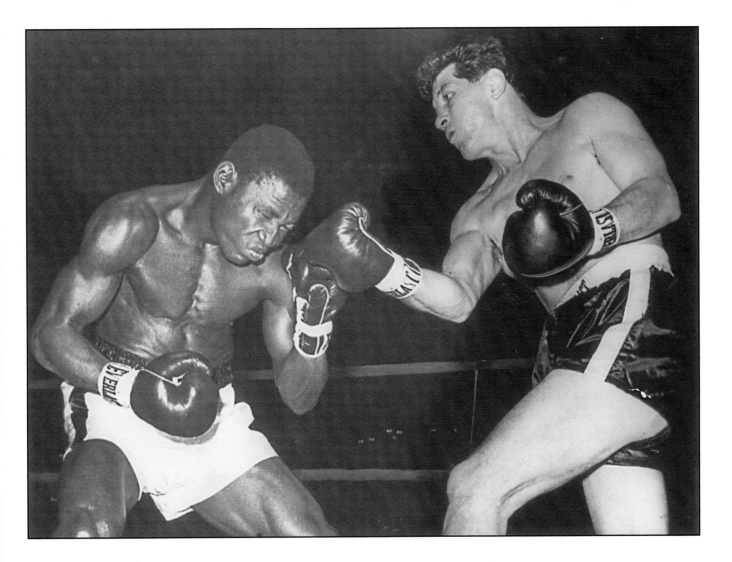

Dick Tiger closes his eyes in painful anticipation of Joey Giardello's
right hook in the fourth round at Atlantic City. Giardello went on
to win the middleweight title. (UPI/Corbis photo)

# GIARDELLO'S TITLE A MEMORIAL TO DAD

DECEMBER 7, 1963
BY LARRY MERCHANT

Joey Giardello had been middleweight champion of the world for 50 minutes. About 30 of those minutes were spent in the ring in Convention Hall, Atlantic City, and maybe 20 of them were a part of his fight with Dick Tiger.

By the 11th round, Tiger no longer was defending the title: Giardello was. He was leading from South Philadelphia to Nigeria.

Only a revolution could have changed the outcome by then—a revolution in Tiger's style, a revolution that would have turned him into a real tiger. But this was not in the man. He has one speed: stalk. He stalks you, in a half shell, hoping to catch you on the ropes, or anywhere else, and beat you down with his strength.

He could not catch Giardello because he didn't chase him hard enough—hard enough to tire him later in the fight—and, of course, Giardello was not going to stand there with him. He stood outside and popped him. He stood on legs that had gone 15 rounds once in 15 years at this business, and if that's the way Tiger was going to fight, beautiful. Like Clyde Beatty with a chair, a whip and a gun loaded with blanks. Giardello would fend him off, while piling up points with a loud and busy left and a louder but only occasional right.

It was after the 12th round that the thing first came up, said Arnold Giovanetti, Giardello's advisor. "He knew he had it," Giovanetti said. "There were tears coming down his cheeks. He said, 'I'm doing this for my dad.'"

Now it was after Giardello had been champion, officially and unofficially, for 45 minutes and it came up a second time. "I'm sorry my dad didn't see it," he said. "He should have seen me do it in 1954, but I didn't give it to him."

The significance goes back to his jail sentence for assault in 1954. His father, Joe Tilleli, who had fought under the name Ed Martin, died during the four months Giardello was at Holmesburg.

"They brought Joey to the wake in Brooklyn," says Giardello's brother Bob Tilleli. "The guards stood outside. Joey went over to the casket and swore on it that he would win the championship some day."

The chance came because Giardello, dedicated to making good his oath, took the fight for practically nothing in terms of money (which explains why he has always been a sucker for the shortest of short ends if he thought it would lead to a title match). Giardello seized the chance and never let it go because there was more emotion involved even than the above, but closely related to it—and to the remark of his newly earned cleanliness.

To Giardello the championship is a prize big and glittering enough to bury for all time the dark side of his past.

Joe Frazier heads for a neutral corner as a
dazed Muhammad Ali struggles to stand.
(Daily News photo by Elwood P. Smith)

# JOE'S SMOKE PUTS OUT ALI'S FIRE

MARCH 8, 1971
BY TOM CUSHMAN

A decade of babble, of swirling motion and emotion, of noise that sometimes became deafening. And then, suddenly, silence.

The legend of Muhammad Ali came tumbling down in Madison Square Garden with 20,455 witnesses and a fair portion of the theater-going world looking on. Joe Frazier, who learned his trade in the grimy, head-knocking atmosphere of Philly's gyms, provided the push. Not spectacularly, but—rather—in Frazier fashion. Grim, relentless and no quarter given.

What happened is that Joe Frazier whipped Muhammad Ali in the one way most people agreed he couldn't, over 15 rounds of magnificent prizefighting. Joe did it like a man climbing the mountains, grunting and puffing and struggling but never taking his eyes off the peak. He couldn't put his man away like he said he would, so he took him apart. And in one breathless instant during the 15th and final round, he sent the left hook soaring home like a demolition ball.

The ratio of cheers and boos for each was rated, roughly, a draw. At times during the night, chants of "Ali-Ali-Ali" swept through the crowd, only to be answered by "Joe-Joe-Joe" being chorused by the other side. Feelings were strong.

They were in the ring, too. You didn't get far into this fight before you began to realize that these guys don't like each other—really. No put-on.

All through the night the byplays continued. A minute into the fight Frazier sank his first hook to the body. And Ali turned to the crowd, shaking his head,

assuring everybody it was nothing. Unfortunately, he was not available an hour later to edit the impression.

Then 25 seconds into the 15th, Frazier double-hooked for one of the few times during the evening. The first struck Ali on the elbow, the second nearly put his head in the mezzanine. Ali went down as if somebody had jerked the ring out from under him. He was up at two, however, waited out the eight, and finished the round—mostly courtesy of Frazier, who was already celebrating. He had to know the knockdown was only a punctuation mark.

"I feel stronger than I did when I went in," Joe told the assembly of writers some 10 minutes later, peering from beneath swollen eyes.

"I want him to come to me and apologize for all the things he called me," Frazier added. "He mumbled something after they announced the decision but I couldn't understand. I didn't make him crawl across the ring like he said he would."

Then Frazier told it like everybody had seen it. "I got to give him credit," Joe sighed. "He takes some punch. That last shot I hit him with, I reached all the way back home for."

Rematch: "I don't think he'll want one," Frazier said. "And me and Yank [Durham], we got to go home and take it easy for a while. I've got to live a little. I've been working 10 years for this night."

So had the other guy, and what it fetched him was an ugly jaw and a loss a lot of people thought never would come. "God knows I whipped him," Joe said.

God knows he surely did.

David Reid reacts to winning the gold medal in a bout against
Alfredo Duvergel of Cuba at the 1996 Summer Olympics in
Atlanta. At left is U.S. assistant coach Patrick Burns.
(AP/Wide World Photos/Kathy Willens)

# ONE PUNCH, ONE GOLD MEDAL
## REID KOs CUBAN IN THIRD ROUND

AUGUST 4, 1996
BY RICH HOFMANN

The right hand came from someplace in downtown Augusta. Down by 10 points entering the final round, down by 10 points to Cuba's Alfredo Duvergel, David Reid had no choice but to reach back that far. His other options were gone.

He fancies himself a boxer, Reid does. His jab has been splendid throughout this Olympic boxing tournament in Atlanta. But there was no time left for pretty, or nice. There were three minutes left—for this 22-year-old from North Philadelphia and for an American team that was in danger of going without gold for the first time since 1948.

And then came the right hand. Long. Murderous. It might not have been the best punch Reid threw in this tournament, but it's the only one anyone will remember. It knocked the Cuban on his face. Duvergel had trouble getting to his knees, then looked a bit shaky as he got to his feet. The referee took one look and stopped the fight. It was 35 seconds into the third round.

Reid took the gold.

The United States avoided a shutout.

"Oh, man," Reid said later. "It means a whole lot. I don't want to share it with you all. I'm going to wait until I get back to my room. Then I'm probably going to jump through the ceiling."

Watching at ringside was Muhammad Ali. On Saturday night, Ali was given a gold medal by International Olympic Committee president Juan Antonio Samaranch to replace his long-lost gold from the 1960 Olympics in Rome. After the fight, Reid met Ali for the first time. "He said, 'You're a bad boy,'" Reid said.

"We'd been through this plenty of times," said Al Mitchell, the U.S. coach who has developed a father-son relationship with Reid since first working with him as an 11-year-old at the rec center at 26th and Jefferson.

"If you want a guy in that spot, you want Dave," Mitchell said. "I told him, 'Just go for the knockout. You can't go any other way.'"

"When he went down, I saw him try to get up and he fell again, and that's when I knew he was hurt," said Reid, who leaped in what must have been a combination of celebration and amazement when the punch landed.

"You've got to understand," Mitchell said. "They're Cubans. They want to kick the Americans' tail. They want to do it and do it with class."

When it was over, Reid hugged Mitchell and then circled the ring waving a small American flag, á la George Foreman in 1968.

"I'm a grassroots coach," Mitchell said. "I'm hard core. It's hard for me to cry. But tears went in my eyes. He made the Olympics for me . . . He threw that right hand, and it was my own son."

And in the corner?

"I told him I love him," Mitchell said.

"I've put myself right there, right there with the champions who won gold medals—George Foreman, Joe Frazier, Ali," Reid said. "It's a very special moment."

Julius Erving battles on the boards with a fierce rival, Boston's
Larry Bird. (Daily News photo by George Reynolds)

# A
# CENTURY OF PRO
# BASKETBALL

BY PHIL JASNER

P at Croce looks back to 1983 and sees a parade. The 76ers' president looks hard into the indeterminate future and swears he sees another one. If only his team can figure out how to get there. Sometime early in the 21st century? If you're going to dream, why not dream big?

Philadelphia, a cradle of professional basketball, has yielded four NBA champions in the 20th century. The fans have seen the best team ever, the 1966-67 Sixers, and the worst ever, the '72-73 Sixers. They have seen the game at its brightest and best and at its almost nadir.

They've seen the 7-1 Wilt Chamberlain cast an unparalleled shadow on the sport, forcing rules to be changed, parameters to be expanded. They've seen Julius Erving, who was Michael Jordan before there was a Michael Jordan. They've seen Moses Malone, Billy Cunningham, Hal Greer, Paul Arizin and

Charles Barkley, all named among the top 50 to play in the league, as was Erving. They've seen Earl Monroe, who grew up here but played in other cities, placed on that list.

They've seen Chamberlain force a trade to the Los Angeles Lakers. They've seen Malone and the No. 1 pick in the draft traded away on the same dark day. They've seen Barkley sent to Phoenix in the next-worst dismantling of the franchise. They've seen ownership go from Eddie Gottlieb to Irv Kosloff and Ike Richman to F. Eugene Dixon to Harold Katz to the Comcast Corp.

This hasn't been a city that has won a lot of championships, but with its pantheon of plays and players, it has been a city like no other.

Today, J.W. Erving is an executive with the Orlando Magic and its parent company, RDV Sports. But in 1976, the year the Sixers spent $6.6 million to

Moses Malone holds a broom, symbolic of the Sixers'
sweep, as he enters the Vet after a Center City parade.
(Daily News photo by Michael Mercanti)

acquire him from the New York Nets of the defunct American Basketball Association, he was not merely Julius Erving, but Doctor J.

"Doctor J was an alter ego, an entertainer, an innovator, a regular high-wire act, suddenly set free from the confines of being an amateur," Erving recalls. "It was a mission he was on, and for the most part he accomplished his goals, exceeded his own expectations.

"I never introduced myself as Doctor J. I was Julius. But even now, I hear, 'Didn't you used to be Doctor J?' I get a kick out of that. I had a lot of fun being that character.

"We rekindled interest, we provided hope," Erving says, preferring to remember it his way. "I bought into that. Our uniforms were red, Boston's were green. I was ready to bleed red. You need that loyalty and commitment to survive in Philadelphia. You can't fool fans who live and die with you. I wasn't a mercenary; I always felt part of the family. I still feel that way."

Pat Williams was very much trying to get the Sixers on "Sports Center," or whatever the equivalent was in the pre-ESPN era. He was an executive with the Sixers in 1968 and 1969, then again from 1974 to 1986, before he left to help bring an expansion franchise to Orlando.

"When I first arrived, the organization consisted of five full-time employees, and I saw how hard it was to sell tickets," says Williams, now a senior executive vice president with RDV Sports and the Magic.

The city's passion was for the Eagles, the Phillies and the Flyers, then the Sixers.

"But take a look at Philly's history. Joe Fulks to Paul Arizin. Neil Johnston to Tom Gola. Wilt and Guy Rodgers. Billy Cunningham, Hal Greer, George McGinnis, Julius, Moses, Darryl Dawkins, Charles Barkley, Iverson. That's more than most cities. Look now, they have a new building, strong ownership, a breathtaking new talent in Iverson. The future is as bright as it's ever been. Maybe for the first time, the city is ready to give the team its heart," says Williams.

The parade in '83 wound down Broad Street to Veterans Stadium. The flatbed truck carrying reporters threw a tire in the first few blocks and literally clattered the rest of the way. Lord help anyone trying to take notes.

A few days later, the team trooped to the White House, where President Ronald Reagan had been briefed enough to know that it was rookie center Mark McNamara's birthday.

Maybe that's what Pat Croce thinks about when he looks back and sees a parade. And what he sees in his mind's eye as he looks hungrily ahead, to sometime in the indeterminate future. He swears he'll bring the Sixers to a parade. It's up to us to bring the passion. And the confetti. The memories are already there.

---

An Arena crowd of 8,221—5,000 were turned away—watched as Howie Dallmar's 15-foot one-hander was the difference as the Warriors topped the Chicago Stags, 82-80, to win the first title in the history of the NBA, then known as the Basketball Association of America.

Native son Wilt Chamberlain, who had headed West with the Warriors, returned to Philadelphia via a trade on Jan. 15, 1965, having been dealt for three players and cash. Although he'd be gone in 3 $\frac{1}{2}$ seasons, his mark on the franchise would be indelible.

Always ready to shoot the ball, Joe Fulks sets a new scoring mark.
(Photo from The Philadelphia Inquirer collection)

# FULKS SETS NEW SCORING MARK AS WARRIORS WIN

FEBRUARY 10, 1949
BY ED DELANEY

The enemy recognized Mr. Basketball on the Arena court last night, for every member of the Indianapolis Jets, including their coach, Burl Friddle, had the glad hand for Joe Fulks when he made professional basketball history.

After Fulks had dented the twines with his 63rd point in the Warriors' 108-87 victory, all the Jets gave him a hand clasp as he left the court and Friddle came to the Warriors' bench to congratulate the locals' scoring wizard.

Fulks' sensational scoring spree, accounting for 27 field goals and nine conversions from the foul line, was a treat in itself.

But the great sportsmanship of the entire Indianapolis squad impressed a small but enthusiastic crowd.

His record-smashing feat, which wiped out George Mikan's Basketball Association of America record of 48 points in one game, was the big factor in the breaking of six league marks.

Joltin' Joe figures in four of them.

First, of course, was in individual point production.

Secondly, his 33 points in the second half erased Carl Braun's performance of 31 points made on Dec. 7, 1947, against the Providence Steamrollers, from the books.

Thirdly, Joe's 27 field goals bettered by nine for one game a mark held jointly by Fulks, Braun and Mikan.

Then to climax his great performance, Fulks' 56 field goal attempts were one more than his own standard.

The game was all Fulks. He got 15 points in each of the first two periods and then came up with 19 in the third quarter and 14 in the last.

Fulks left the court with a minute to play remaining and cheers re-echoed throughout the Arena.

Fulks' season total is now 1,196 points in 46 games for an average of 26 tallies a game.

Fandom sensed Joe was "on," as the din of the game's opening whistle died away.

He made four of his first five shots and at halftime had 13 double-deckers on 25 attempts.

Coach Eddie Gottlieb used his entire squad in the rout of Indianapolis, which only this past Monday scored a 17-point triumph over the locals at Indianapolis.

It was a sideshow, with Fulks as the ringmaster, and the crowd went all out for his performance.

Indianapolis made a game of it for the first few minutes. That's all. The score was deadlocked three times, but after the Jets had knotted the count at 9-all, Fulks hit from under the hoop and it was a runaway from that point on.

The game was all Joltin' Joe and it mattered not who scored other points. Fans wanted Fulks to take every shot. An impossible task, indeed.

But they were more than satisfied when Fulks came up with his record-smashing feat.

Wilt Chamberlain gets ready to score on his opponent.
(Photo from the Daily News collection)

# WILT'S RECORD 55 REBOUNDS NOT ENOUGH

### NOVEMBER 24, 1960
### BY JACK KISER

Everything's normal in the NBA. St. Louis heads the Western Division by a few comfortable strides; Boston is back on top in the Eastern family by a few big breaths; and nobody's dunked a foul shot yet.

Wilt Chamberlain did practically everything but dunk a foul shot at Convention Hall last night. He hit 34 points and broke the league rebound record.

Chamberlain latched onto 55 rebounds to shade Bill Russell's old standard of 51 in a 132-129 loss to Boston. Wilt got only four of 10 foul shots and probably would have been tempted to dunk a few, except for one thing.

The dunking of a foul shot is now illegal in the NBA.

Jocko Collins, supervisor of officials, made this ruling Wednesday after a story appeared in the *Daily News* that Wilt might try this form of foul shooting.

"It never occurred to me that anyone would try such a thing," Jocko said. "In fact, it had never occurred to me that anyone in this league would do it. But it would just be too much. Having a man shoot dunks for foul shots would be ridiculous. So I informed officials as soon as I read the story that it would be illegal. And I'm going to inform all coaches, too. We can't change the rule book this year, but I'm going to send a directive out to make it illegal."

So for the second time in Wilt's career, the rules were changed even before he attempted to dunk a foul shot. The NCAA did it years ago when it heard that Wilt was practicing the shot.

Now, if they'll just find a way to outlaw Mr. Sam Jones' one-hand popper.

That was the principal villain in last night's contest witnessed by an SRO audience of 11,003 disappointed customers.

Jones found the nets for 14 points in the final period to pull the Celtics from behind and into a more comfortable edge in the Eastern Division race.

They finally took the lead at 116-114 when the Warriors went stone-cold and Jones went white-hot for a five-minute stretch. Before the Tribe could get organized, it was 124-115, and the Tribe couldn't catch up.

"It was just one of those things," Warrior coach Neil Johnston shrugged. "I didn't get a good game from my bread-and-butter man (motioning to Paul Arizin) and they hit the big baskets. We played our best game in weeks, but it wasn't good enough. We made too many mistakes during that cold stretch."

Arizin scored 17 points, but hit on only five of 20 attempts from the floor. He was felled early in the game by an unidentified Celtic's shoulder but refused to use it as an excuse. "I was just off."

Chamberlain didn't know he had set a new rebound record until informed by a reporter a half hour after the game. "I know that I had 31 the first half," he said, "but I forgot all about any record. I was too busy trying to win the game. If we won, I'd feel good about the record. Now, I don't feel a thing."

Wilt Chamberlain is congratulated by fans and teammates in
Hershey, Pa., after he scored 100 points against the New York
Knickerbockers. (AP/Wide World Photos/Paul Vathis)

# A NEW PEAK FOR WILT...
# 100 POINTS!

MARCH 2, 1962
BY JACK KISER

Writing the most fantastic chapter to an already unbelievable career, 7-2 center Wilt Chamberlain made a complete shambles of the NBA record book as the Warriors defeated New York, 169-147.

Chamberlain, the John Glenn of the basketball set, shattered no fewer than nine of his league records in an out-of-this-world performance in which he scored 100 points.

The Knicks did their best to stop him, or at least slow him down. They played five men on him at times, not even attempting to cover anyone else in the last four minutes. They fouled Warriors guards as they were bringing the ball upcourt to keep them from hitting Wilt. And they tried to freeze the ball every chance they got during the final six minutes. None of the strategy worked.

He made some long jumpers from 25-30 feet out with two or three men clinging onto his wiry, 260-pound frame. Power-packed dunk shots when he had to bull through, around and over a tight knot of defenders. Blazing speed that carried him downcourt for layups after he had launched the fast break with a rebound himself. He earned every point.

Chamberlain's 100th point came with 46 seconds remaining when he outleaped two defenders to spear a lob pass from Joe Ruklick and slam it through the nets. Then all Hades broke loose.

Hundreds of spectators stampeded onto the court, slamming him on the back, shaking his hand and yelling like they'd just scored the 100 points themselves. His teammates leaped up and down on the court, throwing clenched fists into the air and cheering. It took two minutes to clear the court and finish out the game.

Chamberlain, who hides his feelings better than the next guy, couldn't mask his happiness. A wide smile creased his perspiration-covered face as he greeted his congratulators afterward.

"Man, oh man," he gushed. "I honestly never thought I'd ever score a hundred. Never in my wildest dreams. But it wasn't all me. The rest of the team put as much of an effort into it as I did. They had to do the hard work. If they hadn't wanted it as much as I did, then I'd never have come close."

Did he think he'd ever top this figure?

"I'd hate to try it," he admitted with a long sigh. "When that 100th point went in, I was just thinking, 'Now I can stop running up and down this court like a fool.' I'm glad it's over. When everybody's pulling for you like that, then you don't want to let them down. They were with me and the team was with me and that's what made it great. I just don't want somebody to come up to me tomorrow and ask me when I'm going to score a hundred and 20. Scoring a hundred once is enough for me."

Chet Walker drives past Boston's "Mr. Defense," Bill Russell,
for two points. (Daily News photo by W. R. Everly III)

# BOSTON IS DEAD!...
# LONG LIVE THE 76ERS!

APRIL 11, 1967
BY JACK KISER

It was a long time coming, but it was worth the wait.

A decade of bitter, pent-up frustration was washed away in a flood of delirious joy at Convention Hall as the 76ers sledgehammered Boston, 140-116, to end the longest dynasty in sports history.

Some 14,000 lucky ones were on hand to see Wilt Chamberlain and Wally Jones and Hal Greer and Chet Walker and Luke Jackson and Billy Cunningham and Matty Guokas bury the proud Celtics.

It was a delicious night. The City of Losers had produced a winner. A fantastic winner, maybe the greatest in sports history.

It took a fantastic team to beat the Celtics, because champions die hard, and this was a win-or-death game for them. One more 76er victory and this best-of-seven series would be over, and there hasn't been a playoff finals in 10 years that didn't include the Celtics. Nine of those produced championships for Boston, the last eight in a row, and you don't give up a tradition like this without digging in until your toenails ache.

The Celtics came out blazing just like you knew they would. John Havlicek and Larry Siegfried and Sam Jones and Bailey Howell couldn't miss from outside, and Bill Russell couldn't miss a rebound. And Boston was up by 8-0 before the 76ers knew what hit them.

This pattern continued for 17 minutes, and by that time, the Celtics had built up a 53-37 advantage that shocked the rafters-hanging crowd into stunned silence. At that point it looked like another decade of frustration was in the future.

But then the 76ers started coming back. Slowly at first, as Walker and Greer and Chamberlain combined efforts to slice the halftime deficit to 70-65.

Then Wally Wonder stepped front and center to take command and began measuring the Celtics for a coffin. In the first half this little firecracker of a guard had sputtered through a 1-for-7 shooting slump and compounded the woes with three personal fouls.

But now he began flaming.

A 20-foot jumper from the left . . . an 18-footer from the right . . . a driving layup on a fast break . . . another 20-footer from left-center . . . a 25-footer from the right side . . . a 15-footer from the key . . . a behind-the-back dribble around Sam Jones and a 10-footer . . . and another jumper from right center.

You had to see it to believe it. Every shot he took looked like a desperation heave, and eight of nine went in. Sixteen points in six minutes and 22 seconds and now the 76ers finally had caught up. The crowd was going wild and the Celtics were just going, period. The Celtics got in their last hurrah at this point, zipping through for 10 straight points. But it was a death rattle, and they scored only two foul shots after that.

Later the 76ers uncorked the champagne and spewed it all over the joint and whooped and hollered just like ordinary fans.

"I've been chasing those green jerseys for nine years and I finally caught them," chirped Greer. "How sweet it is, how sweet it is."

Sixers' Julius Erving drives around Lakers' Mark
Landsberger and Kareem Abdul-Jabbar. (Video stills
courtesy of the National Basketball Association)

# DOC LEAVES 'EM DUMBSTRUCK

MAY 11, 1980
BY GARY SMITH

Are there any virgin phrases left to describe a Julius Erving move?

Hell, let's try it anyway. Because with 7:35 left, Julius Erving made a move that sent shivers through the entire game and the entire nation. It was a move that people immediately ranked as one of the Top 5 in the history of Erving, and any move that swoops into his Top 5 should be chiseled for posterity.

It started with the 76ers up, 89-84, and Erving at a sharp angle right of the basket.

He took one hard dribble toward the baseline and then left the planet. There were four problems with this move. One was named Mark Landsberger, another Kareem Abdul-Jabbar, another Jim Chones and the fourth was the black boundary stripe that even includes Erving in its jurisdiction.

He went around the first three in one awesome uncoiling of calf muscles, and now he was floating partially out of bounds, well behind the backboard. Come now, even Erving's imagination couldn't find an escape from this prison of flesh and glass and borderline, could it?

So he windmilled the ball in his right palm to kill time and decide, but by now, even gravity was demanding he stop this nonsense. Finally, the fitting climax occurred. He reached from behind the backboard, he reached from out of bounds, he reached around the flailing snake arms of Abdul-Jabbar and Chones and flicked it up with impossible perfect English off the glass . . . and in, I swear, in.

"I couldn't feel what happened," recalled Erving after the 105-102 win. "It took a funny bounce and went in. I guess I made it do that."

What, a reporter asked, do you call that move?

"A reverse layup," said Doc, and everyone chuckled. It was like calling Kilimanjaro a goose bump.

The effect of this move was like a firecracker in a beehive. Grown writers beat each other on the shoulders and old men produced war whoops their own throats didn't recognize. Paul Westhead's wet hands collided in a time-out signal, but all that did was prolong the carnival from 20 seconds to two minutes. Signs shot up like fists as 18,000 people stood to register their disbelief. "Happy Mother's Day, Mrs. Erving—Thank You for Your Son, the Doctor," said one.

"I don't know how he ever got the ball back in a position to shoot," Lionel Hollins said quietly an hour later. "That was incredible."

Someone asked him if this seven-game series was the summit of his career and Doc smiled yes.

"I don't think anything else in my career compares to this," he said. "I think Kareem and I are in similar situations. We're leaders of our teams in a young man's game. We're kinda just holding on."

Giggles greeted that absurdity, and then another media regiment came forth to ask about the fourth-quarter move.

"I didn't plan it," he said. "A force bigger than I allowed that to happen."

Beg to differ, Doc, but Abdul-Jabbar didn't have any choice.

Sixers' Maurice Cheeks and Andrew Toney
congratulate each other in final moments of win.
(UPI/Corbis photo by Pam Price)

# 76ERS HAVE FINAL SAY

MAY 23, 1982
BY PHIL JASNER

Billy Cunningham says the 76ers are a team without a constituency, a team that will follow its dream in spite of a maddening public. The Sixers purged themselves of the demonic Boston Celtics.

The Sixers made history and avoided history in one spectacular afternoon on national television, winning the seventh game of the NBA Eastern Conference finals, 120-106, and advancing to the championship series.

"It was meant to happen, it was part of our destiny," said Julius Erving after the Sixers became the fifth team in history to win three consecutive playoff series away from home.

They did not—repeat, did not—allow a 3-1 advantage against Boston to slip away. But a CBS audience and several thousand fans who met them at Philadelphia International Airport notwithstanding, they did it for themselves.

"I'm gonna be real quick," Billy said in a cramped interview area in the Garden. "I only have two things to say. No. 1, I want to thank the Celtics' fans for the way they responded to us at the end ['Beat LA, Beat LA']. No. 2, I'm ecstatic for the 12 guys and the coaches, and that's it."

He had coached the Sixers past Boston, beating them in a seventh game of a playoff series for only the third time in the Celtics' history and just the second time on their court, and when it was over, he could not bring himself to share it with anyone beyond the immediate franchise family.

"Part of what we talked about," said Clint Richardson, "was how everybody had counted us out. We decided the only way to change things was to just take it away from Boston, to hold together and accomplish something when no one thought we could. That's one of the reasons Billy took us off the floor after warm-ups, to remind us."

The Garden crowd was prepared with its own reminders, including a group of fans who paraded through the aisles covered with bed sheets that had "Ghosts of Celtics Past" scrawled across them in green.

"It looked like 'Saturday Night Live,'" said Caldwell Jones, "and in a way, it helped us. We came out loose to begin with, we laughed at those guys in the costumes, realized how good we felt, then went to work. We played perfect defense Friday and knew if we could get our offense in gear, we'd have too much for them. We never stopped believing we were a better team.

"Sure, we had been labeled . . . by the fans, by the writers. And I hate labels. But I hold in my feelings, because if we unleash our emotions in the direction of the public, if we say what we really think, then we're 'bad guys'—another label.

"It's the nature of the profession, comes with the territory. You listen, then forget about it. None of it matters as long as you don't get down on yourselves. And we never did that. All we said was, it was gonna be difficult today, but not impossible."

"This series, the way it went for all seven games, proves there are no guarantees," said Maurice Cheeks. "They tried to make history on us. They're so used to coming back on teams, I think they were shocked we wouldn't let them do it to us. We started it, we finished it. We played a great, great game."

Coach Billy Cunningham wipes the sweat from
Moses Malone's brow following the big win.
(Daily News photo by George Reynolds)

# THE PROMISED LAND

MAY 1, 1983
BY PHIL JASNER

He sat in the visiting locker room in the Forum last June and wept, the only time in his career he could remember crying after a basketball game.

He asked only to become stronger, and he did. If anyone had the slightest doubt, Doctor J still can fly.

He soared three majestic times in the final 2:02, on a flight plan that brought the 76ers their first NBA championship since 1967. They reached a height they had never been able to reach, and when they did, they buried the defending-champion Los Angeles Lakers, 115-108, at the Forum.

They didn't just win, they swept, becoming the first team since Golden State defeated the Washington Bullets in 1975 to blow through the finals. They are also the first team in NBA history to lose only one game in the postseason.

"I wanted this team to be remembered," said coach Billy Cunningham, "and now they will be. The players did it."

The players had been here before. They were in the finals for the fourth time since 1977, and in each previous attempt, they had been turned back in six games. Doctor J, among others, had no ring. Now they do.

"I'm glad we played Los Angeles," said Erving, who scored 21 points, handed out six assists and made the most dramatic steal of his career with 59 seconds remaining, scoring on a breakaway and foul shot that gave his team a 109-107 advantage.

"In my 12 pro seasons, there was only one time I cried after a game, and that was right here last season after the sixth game and the Lakers had the championship. Nothing has ever affected me that way, not even now.

"I'm standing here, feeling so strong, so purposeful, so good because I know—we all know—we came the long way, the hard way. As sweet as this is, I can't take it for granted. I love the moment, but the feelings I have are more than anyone could expect. I have nothing but respect and admiration for the people in this room, who stayed together, did what had to be done. Whatever criticism we heard during the season, whatever doubts anyone had, the ones who were with us were with us.

"We saw the flip side first, and it made a difference this time. This team took six years to do this, and even though the characters changed along the way, we still did it better than anyone."

The Sixers scored 22 of the evening's final 30 points, creating a spectacular havoc. With 2:02 re-

The Sixers' bench starts to celebrate during
the final seconds of the championship game.
(Daily News photo by George Reynolds)

maining, Erving flicked the ball away from Kareem Abdul-Jabbar, raced the length of the court and dunked. He scored again on a breakaway at 0:59, then drilled an 18-foot jumper at 0:24 to give the Sixers a three-point lead.

"The jumper . . . there wasn't time to drive, there wasn't time to swing the ball, so I let it fly. It found its way to the hoop. I didn't find that shot. It found me."

They will be remembered for their weaponry, for their versatility, for their depth and for their consummate approach to the five-man concept of the sport.

Moses Malone, who was the unanimous winner of *Sport* magazine's MVP trophy, scored 24 points and tore down 23 rebounds, his best performance off the boards in the postseason. Andrew Toney converted 11 of 12 free throws, scored 23 and handed out a team-high nine assists. Maurice Cheeks shot 7-for-7 from the line, scoring 13 points and making four steals.

"I thought this was a picture-book ending," Cunningham said. "Doc has worked so hard and has come so close, and now it is ours. I can't think of anything else but to enjoy this.

"Tonight was typical of this team all through the playoffs. To come into the locker room at half-time, down the way we were, and have the ability to overcome it, is special. This is all special. These are special people. We played 13 in the postseason and won 12. That's something to remember this team by."

"My hand goes to Dr J and Billy," said Pat Riley, the Lakers' coach. "They really deserved the championship. There's no doubt in my mind that Philly had it all going for them. They really had the incentive. They were in control and had confidence. They're a great team . . . one of the greatest teams of all time. By beating us four straight, they deserve to be the champions."

The players rocked the locker room, emptying bottles of Paul Masson and Cordon Rouge champagne that were sent by Shelly Margolis, a neighbor of Cunningham's.

"Nothing I have ever experienced," said Clemon Johnson, "was ever this nice. We are on top. No other basketball team in the world is better than we are."

Even Bobby Jones permitted himself a whole lot of high fives.

"This is a team in the best sense of the word," Jones said. "We do what we have to do every night. They ran out of things they could do to stop us."

Malone, meanwhile, had picked up a magnum of Cordon Rouge. "Let me have some of this, man," he said, splashing more than he consumed. "I'm so tired, I don't know what to say, except that I feel great. When I wake up tomorrow, I'll feel better. I just told myself I had to control the boards down the stretch, and that if I did, we would win. This is the first time I've ever felt this tired.

"I feel a sense of pride. For the players, for the fans, for Doc, for Billy, for the general manager [Pat Williams], for the owner, for the mayor of Philadelphia. But especially for Doc.

"I remember seeing Doc back in the ABA, saw him win two titles there. When I came to this team, it was to win a title with him. I want to be remembered a long time from now as a guy who played on a championship team with Doc."

And what, somebody asked Malone, did he think the Lakers were feeling?

"The Lakers," he said, "will worry about us next season, too. They might want to put us in a summer league game."

Malone was his own man in Houston, insulating himself from the public. That didn't change in Philadelphia through the season and the playoffs. Will it now? Will he finally let us get to know him?

"Gonna be hard," he said. "I'm gonna go to the parade, jump up on a float, ride a float, jump on a plane and go home. Moses will be gone. But feeling good. For me, for Doc, for everybody. For the whole City of Philadelphia."

Allen Iverson scores against the Pistons and
goes on to win the NBA scoring title.
(Daily News photo by George Reynolds)

# IVERSON WINS SCORING TITLE

MAY 5, 1999
BY PHIL JASNER

Larry Brown hoped Allen Iverson could win the NBA scoring championship "without anything bogus going on or us doing anything silly."

Mission more than accomplished.

On the final night of the regular season, Iverson put up 33 points in the 76ers' 105-100 overtime victory over the Detroit Pistons. That left the 5-11 guard (OK, OK, maybe he's 6-foot) with a scoring average of 26.8.

Iverson became the shortest player ever to win the scoring title (Nate "Tiny" Archibald of the 1972-73 Kansas City-Omaha Kings was 6-1) and the first Sixer to win since the legendary Wilt Chamberlain in 1965-66.

"I'm the scorer on the team, that's why I shoot, not because I was going for the scoring title," said Iverson. "A championship is what I want, not MVP or the scoring title."

One step at a time.

"He represents the city," gushed Sixers president Pat Croce. "If he didn't win, it wouldn't be for lack of effort. His points are necessary to us. It's his record, our record, one more record for Philadelphia. To me, what he has done is amazing, indescribable."

This was the description Sixers forward Harvey Grant offered: "The city hasn't had a player of his magnitude since Charles Barkley and Julius Erving. When I played in Washington, we'd hear about his crossover, but to see it day in and day out, it's unbelievable. Guys hit him hard, he gets right back up. He's fearless. I like that in him. He's a tough kid. Tough by nature."

"I want people to feel what I feel," said Iverson. The last two years, I said I wanted to be here when we turned things around. I wanted to stay with the team I lost with, cried with, laughed with."

At the end, with one last possession, he waved off teammate Matt Geiger's suggestion that he launch one last shot, to try to give himself a little more cushion if he could.

"I had enough," Iverson said. "I didn't want to throw anything in Detroit's face."

"The scoring title is neat—a guy under 6 feet, taking a pounding, now being mentioned as an elite player," said Brown. "You can't give him a better compliment than that. We never shoot the ball at the end [of games already decided]. I'd have been disappointed if he had.

"I told him, get good shots. Anytime he does that, we win anyway. When we get good shots and defend, that's when we win."

Temple coach John Chaney expresses his feelings
about a call. (Daily News photo by George Reynolds)

# A
# CENTURY OF COLLEGE
# BASKETBALL

BY DICK JERARDI

From Temple's 3-1 win over Purple Crescent A.C. in 1894 to the Owls' loss against Duke in the 1999 NCAA Tournament's East Regional final, college basketball has been a cherished part of the Philadelphia sporting culture. Well, maybe not since the win over Crescent, but certainly for most of a century.

Philadelphia basketball is about the big schools. And it's about Philadelphia Textile and Cheyney State. It's about Immaculata. It's about the Palestra.

It's about the "Mighty Mites" of St. Joe's and the national champions from La Salle and Villanova.

Temple and Penn are among the eight winningest programs in the country. Temple, Penn, Villanova and La Salle are among the top 30 in winning percentage.

All of our sports are unique to themselves, but only in college basketball has the city produced coaching and playing stars who became national figures.

Villanova played in the very first Final Four (1939). Since then, every one of the Big 5 schools has played on college basketball's biggest stage. Temple and La Salle were there twice. Penn and St. Joe's once. Villanova has been back twice since that first year.

But no Philadelphia schools have been back since 1985, the year Villanova overcame all odds and won one of the most improbable national championships of them all.

In the 1970-71 season, the Big 5 teams were an incredible 103-35. Talk to any historian and he or she will tell you the Big 5 of the '60s and '70s was best.

It was an era when city basketball was king.

It was before television's money discovered the sport. It was before players could go anywhere and be seen. It was when the Catholic and Public leagues were supplying a seemingly endless supply of basketball players. It was when coaching was as important as talent. It was a long time ago.

Still, nothing really can change the essence of Philly's game. The games against those "other" teams were important. The games against each other were far more important.

With rankings, power ratings, television dates and conferences becoming all important, the essence might have been altered some. Maybe these players don't understand what those players understood.

They hear stories now—of the legendary games and the legendary players. What they can't know is streamers, rollouts and pounding drums at the top of the Palestra. They don't know "Four to Score."

History gets lost in the past. Still, you watch the games even today, and these players, these coaches sense what they've meant, what they mean.

Basketball was invented in Springfield, Mass., and perfected at places like UCLA and Kentucky. College basketball, however, is Philadelphia. That was true decades ago. It's true today.

La Salle basketball players line up after getting off the plane that brought them home from Kansas City, Mo., where they won the NCAA Tournament. Captain Frank O'Hara holds the James W. St. Clair trophy, given to the NCAA champion. Tom Gola, voted MVP of the tourney, is holding the ball. (Daily News photo by Sam Psoras)

# CHAMPION EXPLORERS GREETED BY MORE THAN 10,000 AT AIRPORT

MARCH 21, 1954

La Salle College's basketball team, champion and record-smasher of the NCAA Tournament, the Explorers, brought the NCAA crown into Philadelphia. They were welcomed by more than 10,000 fans at International Airport.

The crowd, officials said, was second only to the one that greeted the 1950-champion Phillies as a welcoming committee for an athletic team here.

Most of the throng had seen the Explorers defeat Bradley, 92-76, in the televised tournament final at Kansas City, which began late last Saturday and lasted until early yesterday by the Eastern time standard.

When the plane carrying the La Salle team arrived, the La Salle ROTC band and a drum and bugle corps struck a spirited song.

The team emerged from the plane, with Captain Frank O'Hara carrying the James W. St. Clair Trophy, which is awarded to the NCAA winner. James Finnegan, president of the City Council, congratulated the squad.

Then the players walked through a solid line of La Salle College students to a waiting bus, which drove the team to the college campus at 20th St. and Olney Ave. The bus was followed by a long line of decorated cars. At the college the celebration continued into the evening.

Among the eight men whose court play won the NCAA crown for the Philadelphia entry, only one will graduate this year—three-letter senior guard Frank O'Hara.

Six of the eight are sophomores. The other is one-man destroyer Tom Gola, an all-American junior whose performances against both Penn State and Bradley in last weekend's championship tournament kept sellout crowds on their feet.

"It looks like it's going to be some time before La Salle is knocked off its perch," one opposing coach conceded ruefully.

"This has been a wonderful year (La Salle's record was 26-4) for us," contends La Salle coach Kenneth B. Loeffler, "and this has been a wonderful trip to Kansas City. I hope we can go again—soon."

The 12 new records and one tie established in the tourney were announced by Walt Byers, NCAA executive secretary.

Six of the records were for a five-game series and were written into the books for the first time, since the 1954 championships produced the first victor that had to go the full five-game route.

La Salle figured in five of the new records and tied for another, including Gola's 112 total points.

In its 26-4 march to the NCAA crown, La Salle won the Mid-Atlantic States Conference title and then defeated Fordham, North Carolina State, Navy, Penn State and Bradley.

Bradley had led through most of the first half of the Saturday-night title game and held a 43-42 halftime margin. But La Salle settled the issue in the third period by netting 30 points in the 10-minute stanza, scoring 22 of the total within a smashing five-minute rally period.

Said Loeffler: "We are happy, indeed, to be champions."

Immaculata's Rene Muth takes a shot.
(Daily News photo by Sam Psoras)

# PIONEER WOMEN

MARCH 23, 1974
BY BERNARD FERNANDEZ

---

*This story was written on the 12th anniversary of
Immaculata's third consecutive national championship.*

---

Even now, after the Immaculata Mighty Macs first crept into the national consciousness on a wing and many prayers, it is difficult to visualize their improbable rise to sporting prominence.

Consider their legacy:

Nationwide participation in women's college athletics has increased from 30,000 to 150,000-plus. More than 95.7 percent of the schools with female enrollments field women's varsity basketball teams.

But this is now, and that was then. It is not unreasonable to presume that the growth rate in women's athletics would have been considerably less dramatic were it not for the foothold gained by the Mighty Macs.

By the third year of Immaculata's reign, the Might Macs, clad in tunics and skirts representative of an earlier era, had gone from playing in front of audiences of less than 100 to a date in Madison Square Garden that attracted 11,969 paying spectators.

"That was the most incredible thing for me personally," said Sister Marian William Toben, president of Immaculata. "To be riding in that crowded bus and looking up at the marquee at Madison Square Garden that said, 'Immaculata College.' Never in my wildest dreams could I have imagined such a thing happening."

The Mighty Macs hardly seemed suited for the role of trailblazing pioneers. None of them had been recruited for their athletic prowess, which is not surprising at a school that did not offer financial aid to athletes. Their 24-year-old coach's previous experience had been confined to a nearby junior high team. The school's approach to sports was that it was simply a device for young ladies to get some exercise.

"Here we were, an all-girls, liberal arts school with no physical education major," said Cathy Rush, the coach who guided Immaculata to the three national championships and two second-place finishes in her seven seasons. "We had no budget to speak of. None of our players had been recruited, none were on scholarship and I was barely older than some of my players.

"You can pick out a million reasons why we

Coach Cathy Rush gives her team some pointers
during practice. (Daily News photo by Sam Psoras)

shouldn't even have been winning, much less dominating. Looking back, I still think it's unbelievable. The odds against everything falling together like it did had to be greater than hitting the lottery."

"In a way, I guess it was the biggest fluke in the world that so many talented players wound up at Immaculata at the same time," said Maureen Mooney, a player on the 1972 and 1973 teams. "It certainly wasn't planned that way, it just happened."

One by one, however, the parts of the championship puzzle began to be fitted. Theresa Shank Grentz, a high-scoring center, enrolled in 1970 along with Denise Conway Crawford. Rene Muth Portland and Maureen Stuhlmann arrived a year later, and along with junior returnees Janet Ruch Boltz and Mooney, they formed the nucleus of the first certifiable powerhouse in women's basketball.

"We all enrolled at Immaculata for different reasons," Mooney said, "but the one thing most of us had in common was that we were used to tough competition in the Philadelphia Catholic League. In a way, college basketball was a step down for several of the girls. We had played before much bigger crowds and in much more pressurized situations in high school."

Grentz, now the highly successful women's basketball coach at Illinois, said she instinctively knew the potential of the group that had been assembled through blind luck. "I remember telling Denise, 'OK, we're not going to lose a game the whole four years we're here,'" Grentz said. "As it was, we almost made it. We lost two games in the four years I was at Immaculata."

Rush was not sure at first what had been dropped in her lap. In 1971-72, her second season, the Mighty Macs went unbeaten in the regular season and earned an invitation to the first-ever AIAW national tournament.

The Mighty Macs won the championship and avenged their only loss in a 24-1 season when they upset favored West Chester by four points.

That might have been the end of the Immaculata story—a shot in the dark that, inexplicably, found the target—except for Rush's dogged refusal to restrict Cinderella to a single trip to the ball.

"Our first championship season, I'll be the first to admit I didn't have a lot of coaching knowledge," Rush said. "What happened, basically, is that I learned with the players."

Making full use of her husband's NBA contacts [Ed Rush, a longtime NBA referee], Rush quickly made up lost ground. She conducted a series of clinics, quizzing the likes of guest speakers Gene Bartow, Dean Smith, Al McGuire and Bobby Knight. "I'd pick them up at the airport," Rush said, "and then I'd pick their brains."

In 1972, their first championship season, the Mighty Macs were about as amateur a group of athletes as you could find.

"When we flew to Illinois for the [national] tournament, I had the only full-fare ticket," Rush said. "We could afford to bring only eight of our players, and they all flew standby.

"We had no assistant coach, no trainer, no sports information director, no statistician. Our girls stayed four to a room and they did their own laundry. Every time we'd play a game, they had to wash their uniform because it was the only one they had."

And now? The NCAA is the governing body of women's college athletics; teams invited to the national tournament presumably do not have to peddle toothbrushes to meet expenses as Immaculata did; and championship-caliber teams no longer are produced by accident. Some would call that progress.

"What happened to Immaculata is almost unique in the history of sports," Rush said. "It was crazy. It was wonderful. And it'll never happen again."

Penn's Tony Price soars for a rebound against Temple earlier
in the season. (Daily News photo by Prentice Cole)

# DREAM TRIP TAKES PENN TO FINAL FOUR

MARCH 18, 1979
BY DICK WEISS

The satellite that Penn's surging basketball team launched at the beginning of the NCAA Tournament has been in orbit now two weeks longer than expected.

Bobby Weinhauer's Ivy League champions soared still higher into outer space yesterday when they defeated St. John's, 64-62 in Greensboro, N.C., and became the first team in a much-maligned conference to reach the Final Four since Bill Bradley and Princeton pulled off the impossible dream in 1965. The Quakers will continue their trip to Salt Lake City against Michigan State. It will be the first visit to the national semifinals in Penn's history, but there is little that seems to awe this group.

"The NCAA is like a huge wave," Tony Price said. "You get on it, ride it for as long as you can, until somebody knocks you off." Price made the biggest splash in the East-dominated regional, scoring 14 of his 21 points in the second half despite playing the final 6:47 of this gut-wrencher with four personals. The Quakers' 6-7 senior captain, who Weinhauer keeps referring to as "the most complete player in the East," also grabbed 12 rebounds and personally pulled the Penn offense together by making all six field goals he attempted in the final 20 minutes. "The way he played for us is typical," Weinhauer said. "He's been a great leader for us all year, a great clutch player."

So the Quakers won by only two instead of four. Their offensive efficiency at crucial junctures only further exemplifies the high control factor on this team.

Penn spent a frustrating 40 minutes trying to up the pace with a full-court press and half-court trap. "We just wanted to run," Price confessed. "But St. John's was very patient. They did a good job of slowing us down in the first half, especially with their zone.

We weren't hitting outside shots and they were just sagging inside. We couldn't get anything going. I missed a lot of chippies then. A couple 12-footers, an eight-footer in the lane. The ball just wasn't dropping. I wasn't shooting the ball out of my range, though. If I had been, it might have messed up the machine." The machine had just enough gas to make it home. Frank Gilroy hit both ends of a one-and-one to give the Redmen a tie at 62, and then Penn went to its delay offense with just 52 seconds remaining.

With 23 seconds to go, St. John's guard Tommy Calabrese was called for brushing Booney Salters, and the 6-1 junior calmly put away two free throws to give the Quakers a two-point lead. There was still a bit of high drama to go, however. Calabrese brought the ball down against Penn's 1-3-1 matchup and found himself open for an 18-footer from the right side. The ball clanked off the rim but was rebounded by Gordon Thomas. Thomas missed a short banker but Ron Plair, the Redmen's slinky 6-4 sophomore, grabbed the ball underneath. Plair, who had made nine consecutive field goals, collided with Wayne McKoy, though, and his follow-up never reached the rim. "I thought for sure we would be in overtime," Price said. "I remember yelling to Vincent [freshman Ross], 'Don't foul!'"

Almost miraculously, Price emerged from the collage of bodies to grab the rebound for Penn. He was fouled immediately by Gilroy. His first part of a one-and-one missed. But time ran out before St. John's could attempt another miracle. So it's on to the Final Four, where Penn, as it has been throughout the tournament, will undoubtedly be considered an underdog to Earvin Johnson and mighty Michigan State.

John Smith gets a hug from a teammate celebrating St. Joseph's win.
(UPI/Corbis photo by Skip Peterson)

# HAWKS' DREAM ALIVE

MARCH 14, 1981
BY PHIL JASNER

Ernest is a confident, strong, young adult. Well established in his profession, as an actor. Well heeled. Macho. He is the central figure in a play called "Impromptu." You would have to have been inside the classroom at Penn State Ogontz five years ago to have seen the production.

John Smith, now the rising young star of the St. Joseph's basketball team, got an A for it.

Smith and his irrepressible, improbable teammates earned another set of exemplary grades on national television, stunning DePaul, 49-48, and advancing to the NCAA Mideast Regional semifinal against Boston College in Bloomington, Ind.

The road to the Final Four suddenly resembles the Yellow Brick one after all, and Smith—now the Hawks' co-captain and weakside forward—is playing a real-life version of the role he created on the Ogontz campus.

"Everybody was trying to get near Ernest, rub elbows with him, find out what it took to get to the top," John was saying, still unwilling to wash away the stars in his eyes. "It's funny, because I identified with the guy. Not that I had exactly made it back then, or even now, but that I wanted to get there. I've studied the character, and I'm not sure he ever was less than a success. Me, I'm just trying to get there."

There are 11 seconds left in what has already been a spectacular reach for the brass ring, and John Smith, Tony Costner, Lonnie McFarlan and Jeffery Clark are streaking up the floor in Dayton, Ohio, trying to fill precious lanes as Bryan Warrick coldly weaves past DePaul guards Skip Dillard and Clyde Bradshaw.

Warrick flashes the ball through his legs, behind his back, leaving the two defenders flailing after him. He stops McFarlan along the right baseline and sends the freshman a swift, accurate pass.

McFarlan, in turn, squares his shoulders to face the basket and goes up for glory. Halfway through the motion, he realizes the only people in front of him are Smith and Costner.

Lonnie drops the ball inside to Smith, who lays in the points heard 'round the basketball world. The No. 1 team in the nation, that quickly, is gone from the tournament. "That's the best thing that has ever happened to me," Smith was to say later, "aside, maybe, from being born."

All this brings us to one final, poignant scene. Ray Meyer, the crushed DePaul coach, is being interviewed, and John Smith—awaiting his own turn—is behind him.

"We stared each other in the eye," John said. "I told him he was a great coach, a legend, that I loved him."

Coach Rollie Massimino gets a ride on his players' shoulders after
winning the NCAA title. (Daily News photo by Rick Bowmer)

# IN THE END, IT'S ALL 'NOVA

APRIL 1, 1985
BY DICK WEISS

They came to watch a coronation. What they saw was a palace revolt.

Yes. Villanova, a team that no one thought had much of a chance to beat mighty Georgetown, became the national champion.

The Wildcats (25-10) earned that title by stunning the top-ranked Hoyas (35-3), 66-64, in front of a sellout crowd of 23,124, in the NCAA championship game at Rupp Arena.

"In the country, I don't think there were more than five people out of 250 million who would have said, 'Villanova's going to win tonight,'" sophomore guard Harold Jensen said. "I'd like to thank those people."

Jensen helped the Wildcats ride home a longshot, scoring six of his 14 points in the last 2:36 as Villanova—which had been to the Final Four twice before—won its first-ever NCAA championship.

Villanova, which had lost to Georgetown twice during the regular season, shot like true winners the third time around. The Wildcats set a championship-game record by hitting 22 of 28 shots (78.6 percent) from the field. They were an incredible 9-for-10 in the second half against a team that led the country in field goal percentage defense.

Earlier in the day, Al Severence, the 79-year-old former Villanova coach, suffered a massive coronary at the team's motel and was pronounced dead at St. Joseph Hospital across the street.

"It's too bad he [Severence] couldn't be with us," coach Rollie Massimino said. "Father [Bernard] Lazor, our team chaplain, made the statement that hopefully Al was somewhere in heaven today, swatting the ball from the basket to give us a shot to win."

Such is the stuff of miracles.

"We were the only team that held them under 60 all year," Massimino said. "Those of you who watched the ESPN rerun of our game with them in Landover [Md.] today, you saw that, with three minutes to go, we were winning and the [45-second shot] clock was involved. We didn't try to hold the ball tonight. We just tried to control the tempo."

The last several seconds were particularly tense. Georgetown had no time-outs and Villanova had five seconds left in which to inbound the ball, so the game figured to be over. But officials stopped the clock with two seconds to go after David Wingate knocked the dead ball into the stands.

Jensen inbounded the ball to Dwayne McClain, who had been knocked to the floor. But Dwayne cradled the ball as time ran out.

That meant the time was right for Villanova's wild on-court celebration, featuring Ed Pinckney and McClain jumping up on the scorer's table.

"Everybody thought Georgetown. Everybody thought Georgetown," Pinckney screamed at the media.

"April fools," Dwayne McClain shouted out.

Yes, Villanova is the national champion.

And that's no joke.

Christian Laettner slam dunks in Duke's 1992 tournament
victory over Kentucky. (Daily News photo by Jim MacMillan)

# DEVILS' VICTORY
# SIMPLY HEAVENLY

MARCH 28, 1992
BY MIKE KERN

An hour after his Duke team had won an absolute Bo Derek of a college basketball game in a freeze-frame finish destined to be replayed forever, Mike Krzyzewski, his tie still perfectly knotted, stood on the Spectrum floor, graciously fulfilling one last interview request.

An hour earlier, top-ranked, defending national champion Duke had won the NCAA East Regional title by defeating Kentucky in overtime, 104-103, on a straightaway jump shot from just beyond the foul line by 6-11 All-America senior center Christian Laettner at the horn.

"I can't provide the adjectives. It's up to you to do that," Krzyzewski had said a bit earlier in the media room. "It was incredible. I guess that's a pretty good one. I'm a little stunned. For a guy who loves the game for the game itself, you hope that someday you can be a part of something like this. And I was. I've just been standing around, trying to figure out what a lucky son of a gun I was just to be involved. I can only thank God."

Counting the five-minute overtime period, there were eight ties and 10 lead changes in the last 10:25. During that span, which saw Laettner get slapped with a technical foul when he stepped on the chest of Kentucky's Aminu Timberlake, neither team led by more than three. And in the last 32 seconds alone, the lead changed hands five times.

Ah, the final 32 seconds. After Laettner hit a difficult banker with the shot clock running out to put the Blue Devils up by two, Kentucky sophomore Jamal Mashburn converted a three-point play to give Kentucky a one-point edge. Mashburn fouled out with 14.1 seconds left and Laettner hit two free throws to put Duke on top by a point. But senior guard Sean Woods answered with a 12-foot running hook in the lane over Laettner that kissed in off the backboard to put the Wildcats ahead for what seemed like for keeps, 103-102, with 2.1 seconds showing.

Alas, that proved to be just enough time for Laettner. After catching a three-quarter-length-of-the-court pass from Grant Hill following a Duke time-out, Laettner, his back to the basket and a pair of defenders behind him, showed remarkable presence of mind. Instead of rushing, he took one dribble, faked to his right and then turned the other way. He freed himself up by stepping back and let the fallaway fly just before the buzzer. The ball fell through the net for his 30th and 31st points. He had scored Duke's final eight points of the contest.

Laettner's game-winner wasn't his first in the searing spotlight of the NCAA Tournament. In the 1990 East Regional final against Connecticut at the Meadowlands, he hit a 12-foot leaner at the buzzer off an inbounds play to give Duke a 79-78 victory in overtime.

"I can't believe it would be an even better feeling than that was," Laettner said, "but it's totally incredible. This was even more fun the second time."

Randall Cunningham prepares to toss his shoe to the crowd after
an Eagles win over the Cowboys at the Vet.
(Daily News photo by Michael Mercanti)

# A CENTURY OF PRO FOOTBALL

BY PAUL DOMOWITCH

In April '99, more than three dozen Eagles fans, some sober, many not, took a bus to New York for the NFL draft. They made the two-hour trip primarily to express their displeasure on national television over the Eagles' decision to select quarterback Donovan McNabb rather than the guy they wanted, running back Ricky Williams.

With all due respect to the Phillies, Flyers and 76ers, this is a football town. Walk into any bar, listen to any talk show, and you'll realize that immediately.

The Eagles have won just three championships in 66 years, the last one nearly four decades ago. But it doesn't matter. They've had 41 losing seasons in those 66 years and have made the playoffs just 14 times. But that doesn't matter either. In Philadelphia, football rules. Bert Bell and Lud Wray knew that 66 years ago when they plunked down $2,500 for the defunct Frankford Yellowjackets and renamed them the Eagles. And Jeffrey Lurie knew that in 1994 when he bought those same Eagles from Norman Braman for $185 million.

"Philadelphia is probably the best football city in the country," Lurie said five years ago. "You have a very passionate fandom here."

The Eagles had a small staff in 1933. There were Bell and Wray and nobody else. Bell handled the administrative duties and sold the tickets. Wray taped ankles and ran the practices. They went 10 years without a winning season before finally turning the trick in 1943.

A year later, they drafted a Honduran-born half-back out of LSU named Steve Van Buren, who would win four league rushing titles in his eight seasons in Philadelphia, and a one-eyed quarterback named Tommy Thompson. The Eagles went from doormat to juggernaut. Notched seven straight winning seasons.

They lost to the Chicago Cardinals on a frozen field at Comiskey Park in the '47 league title game, 28-21. Nothing would stop them the next year, though. Coach Greasy Neale's team went 9-2-1 and won the Eastern Division title, then extracted revenge against the Cardinals in the championship game, beating them, 7-0, in a blinding snowstorm at Shibe Park.

Tommy McDonald is helped by a policeman during
the 1960 NFL championship game at Franklin Field.
(Photo from the Philadelphia Eagles collection)

Van Buren, who rushed for 98 yards on 26 carries, scored the game's only touchdown on a five-yard, fourth-quarter run.

Ironically, Van Buren almost missed the game. When he awoke that morning and saw the heavy snow outside his home, he assumed the game would be canceled and went back to bed. He got back up a little later, though, and wisely decided to go out to the stadium.

In '58, the Eagles made two significant moves that would help vault them back to the top. They hired Buck Shaw as their head coach and picked up quarterback Norm Van Brocklin in a trade with the Rams. The Eagles improved from 2-9-1 in '58 to 7-5 in '59, then captured their third title in 13 years in '60, beating the Green Bay Packers, 17-13, at Franklin Field. Shaw and Van Brocklin both called it quits after the season.

Jerry Wolman, a 36-year-old builder from Washington, bought the team in '63 for $5.5 million. But he ran into financial trouble a few years later and sold the team to trucking executive Leonard Tose in 1969 for $16.1 million.

In 1976 Tose hired Dick Vermeil, a fiery, young college coach who had just guided UCLA to a Rose Bowl win. Vermeil took over a team that had won just four games the previous season.

Vermeil was a workaholic who slept on a couch in his office four nights a week. His training camps were the closest thing on earth to hell, but the hard work paid off. In '80, they went 12-4, won the NFC East title and made it to the Super Bowl. The season ended in disappointment with a 27-10 loss to Oakland in Super Bowl XV. By '82, burnout had caught up with Vermeil and age had caught up with many of his players. Vermeil retired.

The Eagles never went belly-up, but they very nearly left Philadelphia in 1984. Tose was more than $40 million in debt and needed money. He and his daughter, club vice president Susan Fletcher, secretly negotiated with investors in Phoenix to move the team there. Wilson Goode, the mayor at the time, finally convinced Tose to stay by offering him a package of stadium revenue enhancements. Four months later, Tose sold the team to Norman Braman for $65 million.

Less than a year after he bought the club, Braman hired Chicago Bears defensive coordinator Buddy Ryan to be his head coach. Ryan built one of the best defenses in league history and turned the Eagles into a playoff team. They rang up double-digit wins in three of Ryan's five years in Philly, but he couldn't get along with Braman.

After the Eagles lost in the first round of the playoffs in January 1991—their third first-round defeat in as many years—Braman gave Ryan the boot. When Jeffrey Lurie offered Braman $185 million for the Eagles in 1994, or $120 million more than what he paid for them just nine years earlier, he jumped at it.

At his first press conference after buying the Eagles from Braman, Lurie talked of winning "championships." It looked like they were on the right track in '95 and '96, when Ray Rhodes guided them to back-to-back 10-win seasons and was named NFL Coach of the Year in '95. But a plethora of bad personnel decisions eventually caught up with him.

Now it is Andy Reid and Tom Modrak's turn to try to fix what's wrong with the Eagles' franchise. Their first major renovation step—the drafting of McNabb—didn't exactly get a standing ovation.

Three championships in 66 years have a way of making people cynical. But at least they care.

---

Mike Quick caught a 7-yard pass from Ron Jaworski, eluded two defenders and raced to a 99-yard, game-winning touchdown just 1:49 into the extra period of a 23-17 overtime victory over the Atlanta Falcons on Nov. 10, 1985, at Veterans Stadium.

The Eagles' Jerome Brown, a 27-year-old defensive lineman coming off a Pro Bowl appearance, died in a one-car accident on a wet street in Brooksville, Fla., on June 25, 1992. Brown's passenger, his 12-year-old nephew, was also killed.

In the finest offensive performance in their postseason history, the Eagles scored 44 unanswered points to break a 7-7 tie and grab a 58-37 wild-card playoff victory over the Detroit Lions at Veterans Stadium on Dec. 30, 1995. Rodney Peete threw three TDs in the onslaught.

Philadelphia Eagles backfield players Bosh Pritchard (30),
Tommy Thompson (11), Joe Muhu (36) and Steve Van
Buren (15), along with their front line of (from left) Dick
Hermbert, Al Wistert, Frank Kilroy, Alex Wojciechowicz,
Cliff Patton, Vic Sears and Jack Ferrante.
(Photo from The Philadelphia Inquirer collection)

# THOMPSON'S DARING PRESERVES EAGLES' CHAMPIONSHIP

DECEMBER 20, 1948
BY ED DELANEY

A play, perfected at their Lake Saranac training camp this summer, changed the complexion of the game in the Philadelphia Eagles' favor as Tommy Thompson's daring preserved the Birds' 7-0 victory over the Chicago Cardinals in wintry Shibe Park when Greasy Neale's minions won the National Professional Football League title in a driving snowstorm before 28,884 hardy souls, though 36,309 tickets had been sold for this meeting between the pro league's two best aggregations.

The game's only points came about on Steve Van Buren's crunching off-tackle slant from five yards out on the third play of the fourth period and Cliff Patton's accuracy in splitting the uprights for the conversion.

Buttonholed in the champions' dressing room, a scene of bedlam as players and coaches Neale, Charley Ewart, John Kellison and Larry Cabrelli were mobbed by admirers and back-slapping over their great victory, Thompson talked about the play that preserved the lead.

"Under yesterday's conditions, with the aerial game almost out of the question and the footing mighty tough on the runners, I looked for a spot for the play," said Thompson. "The Cards sensed a pitchout to Steve. I faked it to him, held it myself and then sliced through the middle."

It was a daring move. The Eagles backed up to their goal line and picked up 17 yards.

Thompson couldn't have picked a better spot, for it caught the Cardinals unaware. After all, Tommy is a passer—not a runner.

The Eagles ground out three more first downs, two by Thompson, in running out time, and it was no wonder that exuberant fans lifted Tommy, Van Buren and Neale to their shoulders and carried them off the field.

It was a great team victory for the Eagles, as they smashed the "jinx." Chicago had beaten them five times in succession prior. Revenge comes to he who waits, and the Eagles had their inning in their own backyard. Total yards gained showed the Eagles with 232 against the Cardinals' 131.

Van Buren made more yardage himself than the Cards' three offensive gems, as Elmer Angsman had 33, Pat Harder 30 and Charley Trippi 26.

The Eagles tossed away many scoring chances, but they capitalized on the most important one of all. Van Buren hit pay dirt and Thompson finished off the Cards with his great generalship.

No game in the 16-year championship series ever was played in worse conditions. A snowfall which began through the night had left four inches of snow on the ground by kickoff time, delayed 30 minutes until protective tarpaulins were removed. Even the ballplayers were used to help yank the covers from the field.

It never stopped snowing and there wasn't a line visible on the field, which quickly took the slickness of a ski run. Alternate officials were used to judge the sidelines and end zones. By agreement, there were no measurements for first downs. Any measurement would have been impossible.

So the Eagles are wearing the mantles of champions, and one of the biggest heroes is Thompson.

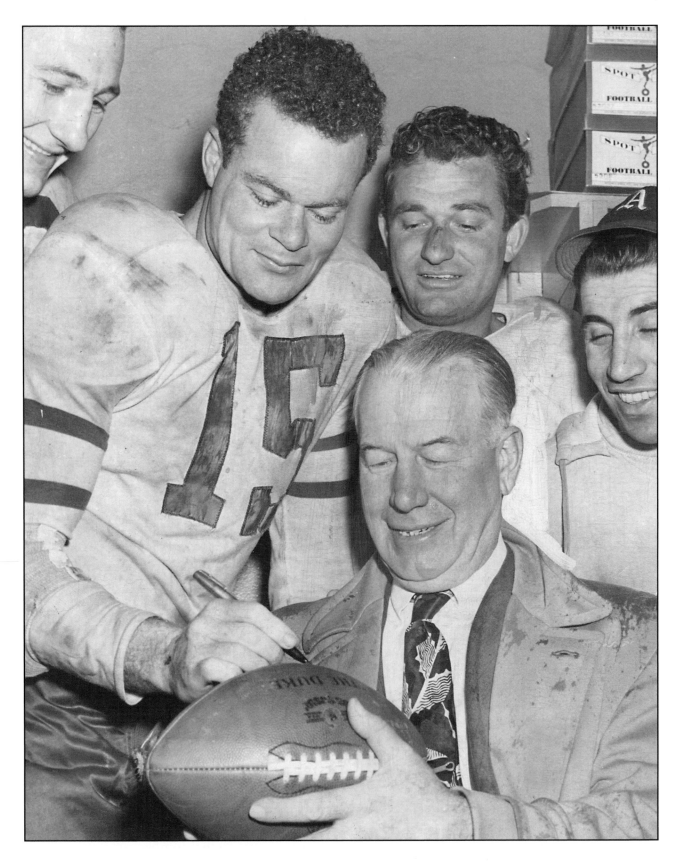

Steve Van Buren autographs a football for Coach Greasy Neale
after the 1948 championship victory over the Chicago Cardinals.
(Photo from The Philadelphia Inquirer collection)

# EAGLES DEFEAT RAMS

DECEMBER 18, 1949
BY ED DELANEY

The invincibility they displayed all season long and the taunts of a hometown crowd against their No. 1 ball carrier, Steve Van Buren, served as the springboard for the Philadelphia Eagles' 14-0 victory over the Los Angeles Rams before 22,245 football attendants in the Memorial Coliseum.

Criticized through the press and over the air lanes as the "Incomparable Van Buren in the East," the "human atom bomb" put on a one-man show as he led the minions of Earl "Greasy" Neale to their second successive National Football League championship.

The precedent they share with the Chicago Bears, who won the league championship in both 1940 and '41 at the expense of the Washington Redskins, 73-0, and New York Giants, 37-9, respectively.

Though they hated to admit defeat to a team that won the Eastern Division title with an 11-1 record, the Coast folks had to eat crow, with Van Buren serving the main course.

Steve was mobbed by teammates when Neale finally gave him the afternoon off with just eight minutes of play remaining.

The crowd sat stunned by such a performance, for never in his career against the Rams had Van Buren played such a magnificent role.

But the tip-off as to what to expect came on Van Buren's sweeps of the enemy flanks. He chewed up much yardage each time quarterback Tommy Thompson either pitched out or handed off the pigskin to Wham Bam.

Even the vaunted Los Angeles forward wall gave ground when Van Buren piled into them and ran over them for precious yardage.

The touchdown heroes in this Eagles' triumph—their 17th in 20 games (counting six exhibition affairs this season)—were Pete Pihos, the Golden Greek, and Leo Skaldany, whom the world champions picked up as a free agent before the Pittsburgh game in Philadelphia.

Chuck Bednarik celebrates his tackle, not realizing that
the Giants' Frank Gifford lies unconscious.
(AP/Wide World Photos/John G. Zimmerman)

# BEDNARIK BLASTS CONERLY
# FOR SMEARING HIM ON TACKLE

NOVEMBER 20, 1960
BY JACK McKINNEY

The nightmare is over for Chuck Bednarik. The New York Giants have given him his honor back, and the Eagles' big all-around guy is grateful for their sportsmanship.

"But I don't see how I can ever have any respect for Charley Conerly again," Bednarik admitted.

Conerly started the nightmare after Bednarik caused the Giants' Frank Gifford to fumble a completed pass Sunday on what Chuck described as "the hardest tackle I ever made." It was in the closing minutes of the Eagles' dramatic 17-10 upset victory and it shut off the Giants' last chance to get back in the game. Although Bednarik insists he didn't realize it at the time, Gifford was knocked unconscious on the play. Later, the New York halfback was carried to St. Elizabeth's Hospital, still unconscious. His injury was diagnosed as a concussion.

"As soon as I saw Frank fumble, I turned to follow the ball," Chuck explained. "When I saw Charley Weber recover for us, I started jumping up and down and yelling, 'We got it! We got it! It's our ball game.' I remember waving my fist as a victory signal. I always do that on a play that means the game."

The next thing Bednarik knew, Conerly was standing on the sidelines, hands cupped to his mouth, shouting, "Bednarik, you lousy cheap-shot artist." In the idiom of the NFL, a "cheap shot" artist is one who piles on, racks a ball carrier when he's hung up or tries in other ways to inflict physical damage after the play.

"How could Conerly call me that?" Bednarik demanded. "I was the only man in on the tackle and I bounced right off after the fumble to follow the ball.

At the time, I figured Conerly was just letting his disappointment run away with him," Chuck added. "I didn't realize till later that he'd be so vindictive."

Later was when someone called Bednarik's attention to Conerly's weekly postgame column in a New York newspaper. The veteran Giants' quarterback prefaced his technical analysis by stating he was "shocked by Chuck Bednarik's antics after he hurt Frank Gifford in the final quarter.

"He stood on the field pointing at Giff and laughing," Conerly wrote of Bednarik's jubilation over the fumble recovery. "It was a disgraceful performance by a guy who's supposed to be an old pro. In this game, you don't injure a man seriously and then laugh at him. For my dough, Bednarik's a poor endorsement for our league and the game of football."

But apparently, Conerly's was strictly a one-man vendetta. In the same newspaper, Gifford was quoted as telling his wife in the hospital room, "He didn't mean it, Honey . . . He had to make the play . . . But it was clean." Maxine Gifford felt justifiable pride in her husband's sportsmanlike attitude. "He was wonderful," she said. "Bednarik was his first thought. Frank instinctively knew Chuck would be charged with a premeditated bloodthirsty deed."

Giants end Kyle Rote also demonstrated old pro class when he showed the game film at the Pro Football Quarterback's Club in New York. The film clearly showed Bednarik throwing a legitimate shoulder tackle at Gifford after the pass completion. "It was just one of those unfortunate things that happen in the rough, tough game of football," Rote commented.

Eagles' Ted Dean tries to elude the tackle of Lions' Dick
"Night Train" Lane at Franklin Field during an October game.
(Daily News photo by David McCuen)

# EAGLES BEAT PACKERS FOR CHAMPIONSHIP

DECEMBER 26, 1960
BY JACK MCKINNEY

Ten minutes of extra preparation helped the Eagles to the lofty title they'll enjoy for at least a year, and Vince Lombardi was the first to admit it.

The astute coach of the Green Bay Packers was asked if he could cite a single turning point after the Eagles came from behind to pass his Packers and then hold them off at 17-13 to win the National Football League championship on Franklin Field.

"Yes, I can," Lombardi answered. "It was that 58-yard kickoff return by Ted Dean. It put the Eagles back in the game, both tactically and psychologically, and we just ran out of time before we could overcome their advantage."

Dean's long return, immediately following the drive that put the Packers ahead, 13-10, in the fourth period, wasn't one of those things that just happen. It was made to happen through the mechanics of a blocking pattern scout Charley Gauer had installed especially for the Packers.

"Ordinarily I don't like to waste time on special kick-return plays because too much depends on the direction of the kick," Coach Buck Shaw admitted. "But this one had special merit and we didn't spend any more than 10 minutes preparing it."

Even before the Eagles put the ball in play from scrimmage, the value of that 10 minutes was evident. Stunned only moments before by the suddenness of the Packers' touchdown drive and by the fluke kick-run option that had triggered it, the Philadelphia offensive unit fairly sprang from the sideline to exploit Dean's penetration.

The Birds needed only seven plays to score the money touchdown and, wonder of wonders, five of them were running plays.

"Our linemen kept telling me their defensive line could be handled," quarterback Norm Van Brocklin explained. "Each kid was so confident he owned the guy in front of him, I decided to give it a try. They were right, weren't they?"

The last word was enjoyed by the man who deserved it most—iron man Chuck Bednarik.

"The Packers are a great team, make no mistake about it," said Chuck, who went both ways at offensive center and linebacker for about 59 minutes. "But after everything that was written about their superiority, we scored 17 points and they scored 13. So what does that make us?"

Only $5,115.55 richer, Chuck, that's all.

With teammates rejoicing in the background, Herman
Edwards takes a Giants fumble into the end zone for a
game-winning touchdown. (Photo by Ed Mahan)

# GIANT WIN FOR EAGLES

NOVEMBER 19, 1978
BY GARY SMITH

At 4:04 p.m. on Sunday, Nov. 19, destiny pulled a violent U-turn. It had spit on the Philadelphia Eagles for over a decade. But suddenly fate made a dramatic swerve and returned to scrape them off the floor and never, ever, for a thousand Sundays hence, shall an Eagle fan have the audacity to curse destiny, bad luck and evil gusts of fate.

Giants' ball, leading 17-12 on their 29-yard line, 31 seconds left. Quarterback takes the snap, flops to the earth, kills the clock, kills the game and kills the Eagles' playoff dreams, right?

Wrong, wrong, a thousand times wrong. By some bizarre, suicidal brain wave in Coach John McVay's skull, the Giants had quarterback Joe Pisarcik handing off the ball to fullback Larry Csonka instead, and what happened next will be frozen in Eagles history forever.

By the time Pisarcik wheeled to make the exchange, Csonka was nearly past him. The ball ricocheted off Csonka's hip, bounced to the turf, skipped off Pisarcik's wildly pounding chest and took one sweet, succulent knee-high hop into the arms of Eagle cornerback Herman Edwards. Edwards fielded it at the Giant 26 and raced home untouched. Coach Dick Vermeil's first reaction was automatic for a man who has been bitten by too many unseen snakes. "I looked for a yellow flag," said Vermeil after the incredible 19-17 win was over, "to see if it would be called back. And then I just felt complete jubilation."

Jubilation and devastation both jumble the brain. Vermeil took a flying leap into the arms of the most unlikely Eagle, Kenny Payne, the player he has been the most critical of all season. Pisarcik laid on his belly and pounded the turf with his fist, like he had fallen on an upturned knife blade. "I don't know if it was a dumb call or not," said Edwards. "When it took that good hop, I didn't think about falling on it. I just picked it up and ran and then looked back to see if a penalty had been called. I was amazed."

"It's about time we had a miracle work for us," rejoiced Ron Jaworski, who had thrown a rally-killing interception just one throat swallow earlier. The miracle ingredients went deeper and farther, stretching 2,000 miles across country, where owner Leonard Tose lay in a Houston hospital bed—five days after top-secret open-heart surgery to replace an aortic valve—listening to the game via special telephone hookup.

With the Eagles out of time-outs, it shouldn't, couldn't and wouldn't have happened if McVay had ordered Pisarcik to just fall on the earth with the ball. "To put it in plain and simple terms, they blew it," said Jaworski. "It was a tactical error."

And one tactical error left its brand so starkly on this game that a whole afternoon full of mental and physical errors by the Eagles was swept under the magic carpet and forgotten.

Dick Vermeil is embraced by Eagles owner Leonard Tose as
Bill Bergey looks on. (Daily News photo by Brad C. Bower)

# BIRDS GO MARCHIN' IN

## JANUARY 11, 1981
### BY BUD SHAW

There was a certain swagger in their walk, a sneer on their faces. Somehow, you couldn't help but remember all those years the Eagles spent limping and wincing like a broken old man. The afternoon was frozen into history. A riot-control squad surrounded the Eagles, but this time it wasn't Santa Claus or Joe Kuharich who'd asked for protection. The Eagles were playing their biggest game in 20 years.

Ron Jaworski flopped on two decades of frustration and smothered it. The Eagles had beaten the Cowboys, 20-7, to win the NFC championship. "It meant so much," Jerry Robinson explained, "knowing there were two minutes left in the game and there was no way the Cowboys could catch up. We were going to New Orleans, the Super Bowl."

Twenty years from now, people will remember every inch of Wilbert Montgomery's 194 yards and every foot of the Eagles' 263 total yards rushing. No running back has ever had 100 yards in a playoff game against the Cowboys. You're supposed to be able to beat the Cowboys by throwing darts at their secondary, but Ron Jaworski was only 9-for-29. The Eagles did it by plunging a knife into the heart of Dallas' flex defense.

They did it with a running back whose uniform was a hospital gown for most of the season. They did it with an offensive line that considered watching films of the running game wearing fake noses and glasses. Montgomery and Leroy Harris ran behind enough blocks to know that none of the Eagles was suffering from hemorrhoids. They sprang Wilbert for a 42-yard TD run on the Birds' second play of the game. Ron

Jaworski would've celebrated if he knew where he was.

"I had taken a shot from Randy White on first down," Jaworksi said. "I thought my day was over. I banged my head on the ground. It was so frozen, it felt like cement. The lights didn't go out on me, but the stadium was spinning. I called the next play in the huddle, but on the way up to the line, I asked Wilbert, 'What did I call?' He reminded me and I just handed off to him."

It became more apparent that the Eagles might be kicking themselves in the butts. They played well enough in the first half to shove the playoff checks halfway into their pockets and it was still 7-7. "We realized it was still 7-7 and that we were 30 minutes away from New Orleans," coach Vermeil said. "We felt like we'd taken everything they had to dish out."

The Eagles' defense cradled the Super Bowl to its breast and never let go. Carl Hairston sacked Danny White and forced a fumble to set up the first of Tony Franklin's two field goals. Jerry Robinson picked up a Tony Dorsett fumble. A couple of minutes later, Harris went nine yards for a touchdown, and it was 17-7. Even the guard dogs were smiling.

The Cowboys had not died a death worthy of America's Team. They were laid out in front of millions of people, 45 of whom now seem to be confident enough to try to make it an annual funeral. "When they come out on top," said Roynell Young, "everything's fine and dandy. But we were winning and Drew Pearson tried to take a cheap shot at me. I'll forgive him but I won't forget."

The Eagles won the NFC championship, and there was a certain swagger in their walk.

103

The Eagles' Wilbert Montgomery runs for a 42-yard
touchdown as Harold Carmichael (17) watches.
(Daily News photo by Brad C. Bower)

# SIR WILBERT OF CAMELOT

JANUARY 11, 1981
BY TOM CUSHMAN

On an afternoon when Camelot was fringed with deposits of white from the winter skies, when the subjects all came dressed in their finest long underwear and sat shivering as they watched the men of Dallas prepare for the joust, it was the young knight Wilbert who ran onto the field and warmed the day. Sore of body, small in stature, but of great spirit, Wilbert darted here and there over the frozen pasture, inflicting grievous wounds, until the men of Dallas gradually scattered, were then routed and finally fled for the plains of Texas.

Those people who value reason above stubbornness realized, of course, that the Eagles had no chance against the Cowboys. Dallas was a team kicking its way across the NFL's playoff stage like a practiced chorus line.

The real Wilbert Montgomery has usually caused grief for the Cowboys' slanting defense, so when the news that a knee had collapsed under Montgomery came out, there must have been enough 10-gallon hats fired into the air to fill the Panhandle.

Wilbert says the leg was quite sore on Thursday, felt better on Friday. On Sunday Wilbert awoke to sunshine, non-Texan temperatures, blue skies and a sensation he had not known for many weeks. Call it a miracle, call it the anxieties of the past few days, some well-disguised con, call it Camelot.

"Guys kept asking me how I felt," he said, "and I could truthfully tell them I felt good, I felt better than I had in a long time."

The Cowboys discovered this on the sixth play of the game, and it ultimately led to a 20-7 Eagles victory, the NFC championship and a trip to the Super Bowl.

Faced with a second-and-one at the Dallas 42, and having just peeled Randy White off his jersey, Ron Jaworski sent Montgomery on a dash through the left side of the line. Responding to the flow with a move so abrupt, the majority of the people in the stadium wouldn't realize that he had started to run left, Wilbert swung back into the alley and said farewell. "As soon as I turned, I could see the end zone," he remembered. "I knew I was going all the way." He did, and with a style that crackled through the January chill like a lightning bolt.

If this is not Camelot, and if these are not fictitious events we have been witnessing for some months now, then how do we explain Wilbert Montgomery limping on Thursday, but running on Sunday like the wind is at his back?

The final score is in the record book. The Cowboys are back in Texas. And the Eagles are prepping for the Super Bowl, which will be played in New Orleans. Which is good news, because it sure is lousy weather here in Camelot-North.

The Eagles' playoff hope vanished in the fog at Chicago's
Soldier Field. (Daily News photo by Michael Mercanti)

# HANGING HEADS
# NOT FOR THE BIRDS

### DECEMBER 31, 1988
### BY RICH HOFMANN

Some will remember Randall Cunningham escaping from Carl Banks on a Monday night at the Vet, escaping and firing a touchdown pass in a watershed victory for the Eagles. Others will carry forever the image of the playoff game itself, of the fog rolling in over the stadium rim and obliterating the second half.

Not me. I'll always see that crowded locker room at Soldier Field, full of football players who looked nothing like losers to the Chicago Bears in an NFL playoff game. There was no celebrating, certainly. But you had to look awfully hard to find the despair that is customary in such scenes. A few jaws were set, but not many. Conversation was easy. Perspective was instant. Griping about the usual (the officials) and the unusual (the fog) was muted. Smiles were brief, but they were there.

Right tackle Ron Heller was typical, as approachable on Saturday as on any Thursday during the season. "I can't deny it—I had a lot of fun playing in that game," Heller said. "I mean, I hurt inside. I'm mad about the way we lost. It's going to bother me for a while. But there's nothing you can do about it now. We talked among ourselves that, win or lose, we were going to make sure that when we were done, we were going to leave it on the field. And I don't think it was a lack of experience. I don't think we choked. Not one bit."

The temptation is to take their ultra-loose attitude going into the game, combine it with the widely held notion that a team has to experience losing before it can win and read their postgame equanimity as the Eagles just being happy to be there, despite the 20-12 loss.

I think we're just trying to reflect on a long season," Keith Jackson said. "We're trying not to let one game destroy the whole thing. We battled together. We overcame a lot together. We won the division together. We're bleeped. Everybody in here is quite upset. We got more than 400 yards and no touchdowns. You have to be upset. But you can't hang on to it. You have to let it go. You have no choice."

Well, now that the future is taken care of, there is one bit of the past to review. Should the Eagles and Bears have played through the fog, or should the game have been stopped? They should have played—bold-faced, underlined, as emphatic as you can say it. Games like this are the kind that people will remember for 50 years.

As for the fog affecting the ability of the teams to throw more than about 15 yards, well, that happens all the time. Two 1987 games at Giants Stadium—the NFC championship game against Washington in January and a regular-season game against the Eagles—were so windy that passing conditions were at least as bad.

Weather affects football. Conditions in January are rarely ideal. Ticket holders undoubtedly would be glad to accept a half refund if the NFL were to offer it. But I'd also be willing to bet that the majority of them will be bragging to their friends next July about what an unforgettable experience it was.

"This year, we were ready for snow, rain, ice," Keith Byars said. "Next year, we'll be ready for fog. Next year, we'll have a fog offense, too."

Eagles coach Buddy Ryan is carried off the field
by Todd Bell (hidden), Cris Carter and Mike
Pitts after a comeback win in Washington.
(Daily News photo by Michael Mercanti)

# 'SKINTILLATING

### SEPTEMBER 17, 1989
### BY TIM KAWAKAMI

It was part triumph, part tragedy, part ecstasy, part providence. It was the day the Eagles spotted Washington a 20-point lead, then simply could not be stopped by the wary, weary Redskins defense. It was the day the Redskins saw the fickle hand of fate flick the football from their clutches just as they were about to bury the Eagles for good.

The game was a four-quarter bloodbath, an offensive masterpiece that, sublimely, was decided by a single Eagles defensive play, a failure by one of the game's dominant players (Redskins running back Gerald Riggs), the ballhandling of a linebacker (Al Harris) and the open-field sprinting of a power-hitting free safety (Wes Hopkins).

"It's the greatest game I've ever been in," said Harris, who recovered a Riggs fumble and handed off to Hopkins, whose 77-yard return set up Randall Cunningham's game-winning four-yard touchdown pass to Keith Jackson with 52 seconds left in the Eagles' 42-37 win. "It was unbelievable." On that single, epic play, starting at the Eagles' 22-yard line, carefully protecting a precious 37-35 lead with 1:16 left, Riggs was about to pound the Eagles' furious comeback into irrelevancy.

Just three plays earlier, he had begun the crucial drive the Eagles' defense had to quench by exploding for 58 yards to the Eagles' 22. Then, out of the clear-blue capital sky, as Riggs entered a pileup at the 19, somewhere in there, somebody, something as of yet undetermined, poked the ball free. It did not roll to a Redskin; it glided straight to Harris, who fell on it at the 19, struggled to his feet when no Redskin smashed him immediately, then got tangled by a wave of Washington pursuers.

"It was just laying there, I couldn't believe it," Harris said, his eyes bugging out in memory. "I fell on it first, and I picked it up and I started feeling people hit around my legs. I know I was ready to go down, and I heard Wes and Todd Bell behind me saying, 'Give it up, Big Al, give it up!'"

Harris shoveled the ball to Hopkins coming up from the secondary. Hopkins spun around Harris, eyed green acres down to the Redskins' end zone and began his long sprint down the left sideline with a convoy of friends for company.

"I just took off and tried to lead him," linebacker Seth Joyner said. "I knew when we were across the 50, I said, 'The game's over, we've got this one wrapped up.'" Hopkins would stop only when he had traveled to the Redskins' 4-yard line, pinched off from a touchdown only by receiver Ricky Sanders' desperate dive. Given the weight of the game on his hands after Hopkins' takeaway and long jaunt, Cunningham immediately zoomed it to Jackson for their third touchdown hookup.

When it was at last over, the shocked, sated, silent sellout RFK Stadium audience shuffled through the exits meekly. "They looked a little upset, didn't they?" Jackson said of the whispering Washingtonians.

And when it was over, there was nothing left for the Eagles to do but collapse and shout aloud, for they had been blessed by a football-field miracle once again. And miracles, unless your name happens to be James David "Buddy" Ryan, do not come by in this world very often.

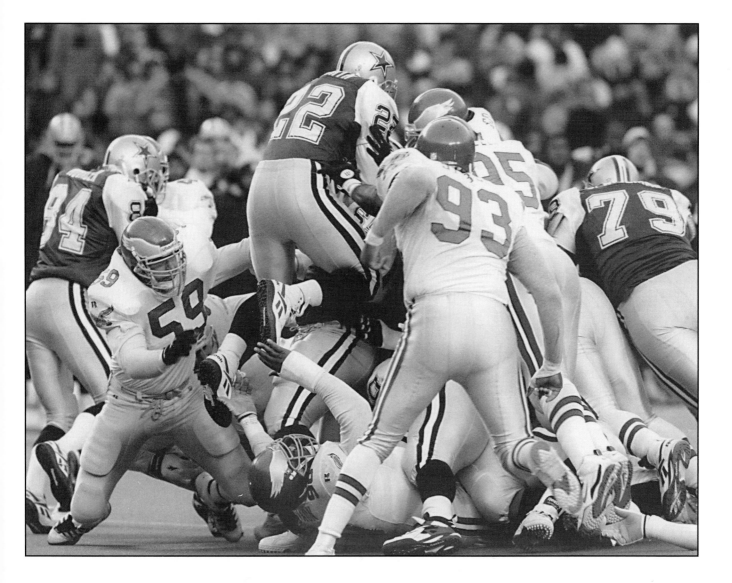

The Eagles stop Emmitt Smith a second time
on fourth-and-less than a yard.
(Daily News photo by George Reynolds)

# THANK YOU BARRY MUCH

DECEMBER 10, 1995
KEVIN MULLIGAN

The Eagles froze for a second, as if waiting for someone to officially confirm that they had pulled off the impossible.

William Fuller had sucked the last gasp from a feeble Dallas offense with a last-play sack of Troy Aikman, but as he lay there, listening to the roar, he could hear no "three . . . two . . . one . . . " followed by a deafening thunder from the 66,198 Eagle fans at Veterans Stadium.

The clock had stopped for reasons unknown at three seconds, and by the game's final seconds, everyone in the house and a national TV audience had learned not to assume a thing, including game over, until the zebras ran off the field.

An entire stadium population was put on pause in the minus-7-degree wind chill. It wasn't fair. Players looked at each other, then the officials, then the scoreboard clock, then each other again. Victory dances were interrupted in mid-step. Hugs of joy became "Wait a second" or "What the . . . "

Then someone realized his mistake, the 0:00 came up and you would have sworn everyone had hit on a progressive slot machine. The Eagles' 20-17 upset of the Cowboys would be interrupted no more.

Crazed Eagles began running and jumping and hugging teammates and coaches; others collapsed from near-exhaustion on the frozen plastic grass. Still others ran for the locker room, fists and index fingers thrust above them.

The South Philly stadium complex became a block party the likes of which have not been seen since the Phillies' 1993 National League championship season.

Another win against the Cardinals, and the Eagles are playoff bound as first-round wild-card hosts. Two victories and they could sneak into the NFC East title picture.

"I don't think anybody in the room knows how proud I am of this football team," said Eagles coach Ray Rhodes.

"It's a great feeling," said safety Michael Zordich, still in uniform an hour after the game. "Probably the biggest win of my career."

The roller-coaster victory ride snapped a seven-game, three-year Eagles drought against the Cowboys.

"To think that we were down 17-3 and came back and beat a team like that," said free safety Greg Jackson. "That says a helluva lot. It says a lot for our

Eagles' Bobby Taylor (left) and Barry Wilburn celebrate after
breaking up a pass intended for Cowboys' Michael Irvin.
(Daily News photo by Andrea Mihalik)

character, our will, our power, our strength and our desire to just go out there and give it all we have. It's unreal, man. I can't believe how hard we played. Unreal."

Few also could believe Barry Switzer's thinking.

Switzer made one the biggest bonehead decisions in recent NFL history, and it might eventually cost his Cowboys the home field in the NFC championship game, and possibly a Super Bowl appearance.

In a 17-17 game. Ball on the Dallas 29. Two minutes left. Fourth down and less than a yard. He went for it! In a tie game. Already in Eagles kicker Gary Anderson's field goal range. At the 29. Fourth-and-less than a yard. Overtime and darkness beckoning.

He went for it! It was more like fourth-and-a-mile the way the Eagles' defense was stuffing Emmitt Smith in the second half. Can you say, "Nine carries, 10 yards?"

"I wanted to make a foot to control the ball," Switzer said. "If we kick into the wind, they're going to come back and kick a field goal anyway."

How's that for confidence in his defense? Most Eagles were stunned by Switzer's move. A few were not surprised at all.

"That's a sign of a team that has a great deal of confidence in their players," Rhodes said. "I'm sure Barry Switzer felt that, 'Hey, we've been in situations like this before and we're gonna take a shot at it and we're gonna make it.'"

Fourth-and-less than a yard. Switzer went for it. Not once, but twice! Same play, too. Emmitt Smith left, led by fullback Daryl Johnston. The first was sniffed out and stuffed for a loss by a gang of Eagles, but it was ruled no play when the refs called the two-minute time-out just before the snap.

Next play, same call, same results. Eagles linebacker Bill Romanowski smashed into Johnston at the line of scrimmage and Smith was dead. Andy Harmon knifed underneath, and a sea of white jerseys swarmed the gap, leaving Switzer as America's most embarrassed football coach.

Then this afterward: "That wasn't the difference," Switzer said. "The way we played for 30 minutes in the second half was the difference."

Nice try, Barry. You blew it.

Three Eagles' runs later, Anderson drilled a pair of clutch 42-yard field goals (the first wiped out due to an official's failure to signal clock start-up) with 1:26 to play.

"It was one of those [no doubt-about-it-kicks]," Anderson said. "I kicked 'em both well. It feels pretty good as soon as it leaves your foot, and I wasn't even watching it [go through]. I knew."

The Eagles' defense—led by rookie cornerback Bobby Taylor, sticking to Michael Irvin—allowed Aikman just three completions in 10 frenzied attempts in the final 1:26. Fuller took care of Aikman on the 11th play, blowing past right tackle Erik Williams to put his personal stamp on the Dallas quarterback, possibly for future reference.

Switzer, it appears, will rue the day he went for it, in an apparent show of disrespect for the Eagles' defense.

"I'm not gonna say anything negative," Rhodes said, "because I'd like to meet his football team again."

And when is the last time you heard an Eagles coach say that?

Flyers' Don Saleski (left) and Bobby Clarke celebrate as the buzzer
sounds to end the Flyers' 1974 Stanley Cup victory over Boston. As
Clarke pays attention to the scoreboard, a fan grabs Clarke's stick.
(AP/Wide World Photos/Rusty Kennedy)

# A
# CENTURY OF
# HOCKEY

BY LES BOWEN

There was a time when Philadelphia wasn't considered a good hockey town.

Maybe to like hockey, Philadelphians needed to experience it Flyers-style. Specifically, 1970s Flyers-style. Rarely has a team's identity fit the psyche of a city the way the Broad Street Bullies fit Philadelphia.

Nearly 25 years after their heyday, whenever things go badly down at the big, new First Union Center, the cry remains the same: "Hit sommmeboddy!"

Let's start with the less-than-promising beginning. The sport's local professional debut came in 1927, as the Philadelphia Arrows took the ice at The Arena, at 46th and Market.

The Arrows played in something called the Can-Am League. In 1935-36 they became the Ramblers, the top farm team of the (gasp!) Rangers. The Ramblers, though, rambled right along for several years. One of their top scorers in 1936-37 was Bryan Hextall Sr., the grandfather of a certain goaltender who showed up here exactly 50 years later.

The seeds of change were planted in 1964, when an Eagles vice president named Ed Snider went to Boston Garden for a Sixers-Celtics game and saw a crowd of people lined up to buy Bruins tickets. He found out only 1,000 were made available on game day, all the others having been previously sold—for what then was a last-place team.

Snider was intrigued and he got Eagles owner Jerry Wolman in on the planning for a new arena that could accommodate a hockey franchise. On Feb. 9 1966, Philadelphia was awarded a conditional NHL franchise. On June 1, ground was broken for the Spectrum. The Flyers first took the ice on Oct. 11, 1967.

They didn't take the region by storm. When they flew home after losing their first two games in Oakland and Los Angeles, 35 fans greeted the plane. Later that season, the roof blew off their new home and they had to temporarily take up residence in Quebec. They got the Spectrum back in time for their first playoff series, against St. Louis, which they lost in seven stirring games.

This setback led Snider to a momentous decision. He didn't like the idea of the Flyers being pushed around. He told General Manager Bud Poile and Coach Keith Allen he wanted bigger, tougher players, an emphasis that began in the 1969 entry draft. A newspaper story noted that "the Flyers drafted seven

Fans line Broad Street as the Flyers' caravan reaches City
Hall during the team's second Stanley Cup parade in 1975.
(Daily News photo by Sam Psoras)

players in the amateur draft, only one of them under 6 feet."

The one under 6 feet was a 5-10, 176-pound center from Flin Flon, Manitoba, named Bobby Clarke, drafted in the second round because of the emphatic urging of scout Jerry Melnyk.

On New Year's Day 1973 in Atlanta, the Flyers won, 3-1, accumulating 43 penalty minutes to the Flames' 17. Jack Chevalier, who covered the team for the *Bulletin*, wrote this about the game: "The image of the fightin' Flyers is spreading gradually around the NHL, and people are dreaming up wild nicknames . . . the Mean Machine, the Bullies of Broad Street and Freddy's Philistines (named after coach Fred Shero)." A headline writer named Pete Cafone settled on "Broad Street Bullies Muscle Atlanta," and an era was born.

Everything came together in 1973-74. In June, the Flyers got goalie Bernie Parent when the WHA Blazers folded, and he backstopped a team that became only the sixth in NHL history to win as many as 50 games in a season, en route to the Vezina and Conn Smythe trophies. They lost Barry Ashbee to a career-ending eye injury during a playoff series with the Rangers, but the Flyers regrouped and won the series in seven games, sending them to their first Stanley Cup finals, against Boston.

Clarke scored a dramatic game-winner 12:01 into overtime of Game 2, and the Flyers knew they could beat the 1970 and '72 champions. They ultimately won the series in six games.

Rick MacLeish scored the only goal of the Cup-clinching victory at the Spectrum, which ended at 5:01 p.m. with the puck on Joe Watson's stick and Gene Hart bellowing into the microphone: "The Flyers are going . . . to win . . . the Stanley Cup!"

As the revelry continued, now GM Allen, already was thinking about winning again. He moved right away to trade for right wing Reggie Leach, who was to be a key figure in the winning of the '75 Stanley Cup.

The early '80s were a time of turmoil as the '70s legends aged and eventually retired. Clarke went straight from the ice to the GM's job in 1984. In his first season in a suit and tie, the Flyers made a surprise trip to the 1985 finals against Edmonton, behind Pelle Lindbergh and a bunch of energetic youngsters led by first-year coach Mike Keenan. Edmonton won in five games.

The Flyers reached the finals in 1987, but fell to the powerful Oilers again, this time in seven games.

After that, the team's fortunes declined. In 1990, the Flyers missed the playoffs for the first time since 1972. The playoff drought stretched to an unbelievable five seasons, mostly because in 1992 the Flyers sent six players, two No. 1 draft picks and $15 million to Quebec for Eric Lindros. He had been drafted first overall in 1991, but had refused to sign with Quebec.

In February 1995, Clarke made a huge trade sending winger Mark Recchi and a third-round draft pick to Montreal for Eric Desjardins, Gilbert Dionne and John LeClair. Desjardins solidified a wifty defense, but the chemistry LeClair developed with Eric Lindros and winger Mikael Renberg was astounding. Their line, nicknamed "The Legion of Doom," was the talk of the league.

Lindros led the Flyers to the Cup finals in 1997, but they were swept by Detroit.

The 1998-99 Flyers seldom saw a dull moment. The '98-99 Flyers were the first NHL team to go more than 10 games without losing (10-0-5) and more than 10 games without winning (0-8-4) in the same season.

---

Defensemen are not normally known for their scoring. Maybe the Cleveland Barons should have relayed that news to the Flyers' Tom Bladon on Dec. 11, 1977. He burned them eight times that day—with four goals and four assists—en route to an 11-1 Spectrum victory.

Goaltender Pelle Lindbergh, coming off a Vezina Trophy–winning 1984-85 season, was struck down in the prime of his hockey career, dying from injuries suffered in a Nov. 10, 1985 car accident in Somerdale, N.J.

The Flyers and Canadiens fired up before Game 6 of their 1987 Wales Conference final series with a 15-minute pregame brawl at the Montreal Forum. The Flyers had taken exception to Claude Lemieux shooting a puck into their net. The teams—with some players rushing half-dressed from the locker room—came to blows that night. The Flyers won the game, 4-3, to capture the series.

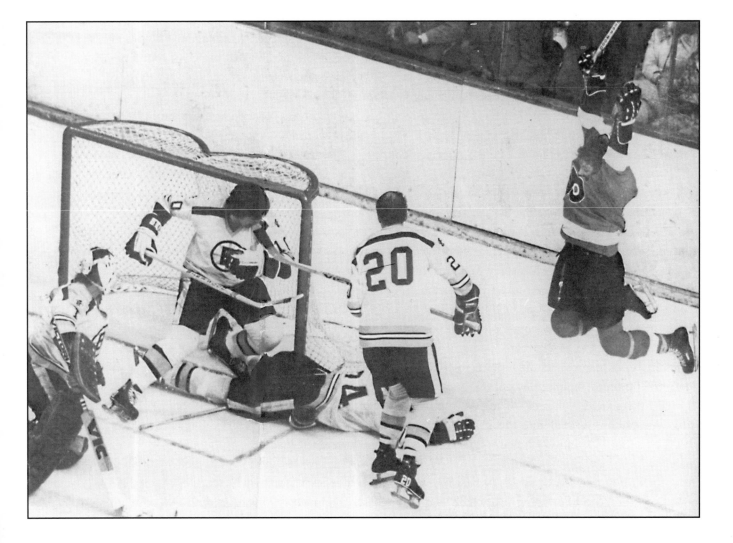

Bobby Clarke celebrates as he scored an overtime goal against
the Bruins. (Photo from the Philadelphia Flyers collection)

# MOOSE PUTS MONEY IN FLYERS' SLOT

MAY 9, 1974
BY BILL FLEISCHMAN

Need a tip on the stock market? Will it rain tomorrow? Just ask Dave Schultz.

"I've got ESP—I said I'd get the winner or two points," the Flyers' overtime specialist said after he set up Bobby Clarke's shot heard 'round the NHL that stunned Boston, 3-2, in a sudden-death thriller at Boston Garden.

Need another dramatic goal? Will Andre "Moose" Dupont do?

All Dupont did was pull the Flyers up by their skate laces with the tying goal 52 seconds before regulation ended. The Bruins were ready to celebrate a two-games-to-none lead in the Stanley Cup final when Dupont scored from, of all places, the slot.

"I was following the play," the big defenseman said. "Clarke was behind me and he was really tired. He told me to take a spot in close, so I ended up as a center. Ricky [MacLeish] was trying to get the puck to Roscoe [Ross Lonsberry], but someone lifted his stick. Ricky got the puck to me and—bing! It was in."

After responding with his most animated "Moose Shuffle," Dupont had a hint the Flyers would win. No ESP, or TWA, or whatever it's called in French. One glimpse at the Boston bench tipped off Dupont.

"They [Bruins] really went down after that," Dupont said. "Everybody on their bench had their heads down. I thought, 'Cripes, if we really go in overtime, we'll win it.'"

The Flyers really went in the sixth overtime they've played in two years (four wins). But so did the Bruins. Two minutes before Clarke scored his sec-ond goal of the game, at 12:01, veteran Johnny Bucyk walked in on goaltender Bernie Parent. Zap! Parent made another marvelous save.

"I saw Bucyk coming on my right," Parent said. "I knew he'd get the puck, and he was coming pretty fast. I just stayed on the edge of the crease and let him make the first move. He faked on the short side, then shot it into my chest."

Reprieved from defeat, the Flyers took advantage of a peculiar line matchup to fulfill part of Schultz's vision. Boston coach Bep Guidolin sent his third line, centered by rookie Andre Savard, against Clarke's line. Schultz, playing his first shift of overtime, fed the puck from the left corner to Bill Flett, who was alone in the slot. Flett passed to Clarke, who somehow was also alone, to goalie Gilles Gilbert's left.

"I tried to shoot it high, but the rebound came right back to me," Clarke said. So he shot again, over Gilbert and a sprawling Terry O'Reilly.

Ironically, Schultz thanked some Boston fans for his appearance.

"Some fan sitting there said, 'Put Schultz on,'" said the overtime goal-scoring hero of the Flyers' quarterfinal in Atlanta. "I said, 'Yeah' and laughed. Next thing I know [Coach] Freddie [Shero] says, 'Clarke, Flett and Schultz.' I turned to the fan and said, 'Thanks.'"

In winning for only the second time in Boston in seven years, the Flyers have convinced the skeptics they aren't on a pleasure cruise toward their first Stanley Cup.

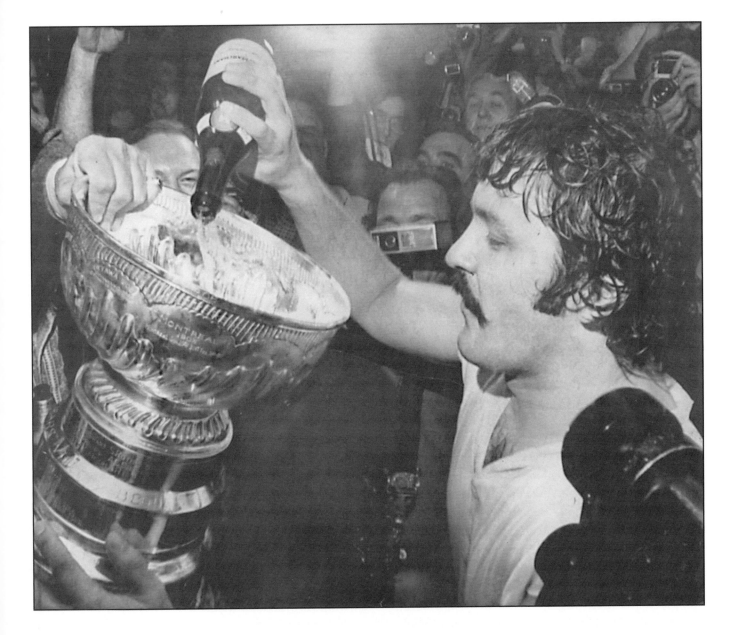

Flyers goalie Bernie Parent pours champagne into the Stanley Cup
after the Flyers defeated Boston, four games to two.
(AP/Wide World Photos)

# BEST FLYERS OF ALL

MAY 19, 1974
BY BILL FLEISCHMAN

Barry Ashbee was on the fringe of the Flyers' first Stanley Cup celebration, a solitary figure observing the wall-to-wall people from behind sunglasses.

"You might never see another bunch like this," the ramrod-straight defenseman said in a quivering voice. "I don't cry much, but I was in tears the last minute and a half. I've never been so proud of a bunch of guys in my life."

Bernie Parent was simply sensational in goal, as he has been all season. A writer's panel acknowledged Parent's performance by voting him the Conn Smythe Trophy as the Stanley Cup playoffs' most valuable player.

Bobby Clarke thinks Parent deserves another award, the Hart Trophy. "If Bernie isn't the most valuable player [for the season], then he was robbed," Clarke said.

Teammate Simon Nolet went further: "The way Bernie played this year, all the trophies should be his."

Parent will settle for Lord Stanley's Cup. "Winning the Cup is a dream," he said after the Flyers' 1-0 victory gave them a 4-2 series win over Boston.

"When you're growing up, you try to figure what it would be like to be on a team that wins it. Now that we've won it, it's not like what I thought. It's a feeling you can't buy or describe."

"I was here with Bernie before and I saw him with the Blazers last year," said Nolet. "I knew he was good, but not this good. When you've got a guy like Clarke giving 150 percent, and Bernie making save after save, if you don't work, too, you don't have any guts."

Bill Clement remembers his reaction to the trade that brought back Parent and shipped out popular Doug Favell to Toronto. "People asked me about the trade, especially after Favvy's great playoff last year," Clement said. "I thought Bernie would help our team with his consistency. He's the ideal player. You know game in and game out what he'll do, how he'll react."

Then Clement, who was still in full uniform and skates nearly two hours after pandemonium erupted, cited another reason for yesterday's perfect ending.

"A goaltender is only as good as his defense," said the young forward who may be lost in the NHL expansion draft. "And our defense was unbelievable, especially the way they played after Ashbee got hurt. Nobody on this team played for himself. Everybody sacrificed. It's so unbelievable, it makes you want to cry."

Bill Clement didn't cry. Neither did other Flyers. Some, like Dave Schultz, kept shaking their heads in disbelief. Others, like Ed Van Impe, sat wearily clutching a champagne bottle and believed.

"It's sunk in for me," the original Flyer said. "We all worked so hard it had to come. The way Bernie played, it was only just for us to win."

Clarke summarized Parent's effect when someone asked about his party plans. "I'll just follow Bernie. I'll walk across the water with Bernie."

Bernie Parent (left) and Bobby Clarke skate with
the Stanley Cup in 1975 celebration. (Philadelphia
Inqurier photo by Richard M. Titley)

# PARENT'S EDGE IS SHARP AS A SABRE

MAY 27, 1975
BY STAN HOCHMAN

"You try to relax, you think about different things," Bernie Parent said. "That's what you call experience."

Oh, is that what you call experience?

Guys were stumbling around the chaos that was the Flyers' locker room, groping for words to describe what they had seen. Parent had turned away 32 shots, some blurs that only he saw, and the Flyers had beaten Buffalo, 2-0, to win the Stanley Cup again.

"He was beautiful," Bobby Clarke said. "The goaltending made the difference."

"He plays good every game," said Ed Van Impe, "and great some games. Tonight, he was great."

"I kept saying," said GM Keith Allen, "that if we had an edge, it was in goaltending."

Some edge. Like the edge on a sword. Or a Sabre. Parent was the difference on a night when the Sabres outshot the Flyers, 13-6, in the first period. They had the power play going four different times and came up empty.

"Scoreless game. Stanley Cup, you don't want them to get the first goal," Parent said afterwards.

First goal, second goal, any goal. Parent pitched his fourth shutout of the playoffs, matching the individual record. Add Wayne Stephenson's shutout against the Islanders and you've got a team record for Cup play.

The brilliant goaltending earned Parent the Conn Smythe Trophy as the most valuable player in the tournament. They have been handing out the hardware for 11 years and Parent is the first back-to-back winner.

"You don't win with one guy," he said. "All season I only had to face maybe 26 or 27 shots. It's a team effort. But, I guess they've got to give the trophy to someone."

He also repeated as *Sport* magazine's outstanding player. That means another car. What will he do with this one? He had no gag reply, but he turned away other questions with small jests. Is he a "big game" goalie?

"A big game," he said. "Does that mean if you faced 30 shots you got to stop all 30 instead of 27? The thing is, tonight, we made them shoot from tough angles."

Tough angles and easy angles and point-blank angles. But nothing got past him. When it was over, he skated a victory lap with the big, gleaming cup, sharing the grip with Clarke.

"It was different this year," he said. "Last year we were in the clouds. This year we had the system. We knew more what we were doing.

"They say it's not the same the second time around. They're wrong. It's twice as good. And what's wrong with three in a row?"

Dave "The Hammer" Schultz looks for a scoring opportunity
during the Flyers' 4-1 win over the Soviets.
(Photo from the Philadelphia Flyers collection)

# THE ORANGE ARMY MARCHES ON

JANUARY 11, 1976
BY BILL FLEISCHMAN

Jimmy Watson's eyes were as bright as a British Columbia moonlit night as he said, "I've never been so happy. This compares with winning the Stanley Cup."

Dave Schultz pounded his bare chest near the heart and said, "We won it right here." Gary Dornhoefer, whose new beard makes him look meaner than Rasputin, said, "It was a gutty performance by 20 guys."

If it sounds like the Flyers felt proud and a bit boastful, you're right. The showdown with the Soviet Central Army, the USSR hockey champions, received more attention than a Stanley Cup final. Or Super Bowl. With worldwide coverage focused on the Spectrum, the Flyers felt they had to win for themselves, the NHL, Canada and Mom's apple pie.

"The fact that they had won the series vs. NHL teams didn't mean anything unless they beat us," said Bobby Kelly.

Well, the Flyers did win, 4-1. The Stanley Cup champions won in convincing style. Even the most skeptical Soviet viewer sipping a 3 a.m. Bloody Mary back in Moscow couldn't deny the Flyers' superiority for this one memorable and controversial meeting.

"They better go home and learn the game," said Barry Ashbee. Ah, Barry, are you referring to the same team that embarrassed the New York Rangers, tied Montreal and beat Boston?

The Flyers' control was clear from the start. The Soviets began with a snappy series of 20-foot passes in their zone that drew oohs of admiration from the supercharged crowd. Then a strange thing happened: When the Soviets tried to penetrate the Berlin Wall at the Flyers' blue line, their attack vanished.

"They could pass the puck all they wanted in their zone," said Dornhoefer. "We wouldn't chase them like they wanted. That and the fact we didn't shoot until we were certain we had good shots were the key to the game. I'd say it was absolutely our best effort of the season."

On Saturday night the Soviet Wings had edged the Islanders, 2-1. Denis Potvin, the Islanders' All-Star defenseman, who served as a television analyst yesterday, said his club was tighter than a vodka-filled diplomat.

125

Orest Kindrachuk begins to celebrate as teammate
Don Saleski shakes hands with a Soviet player after
the Flyers beat the Soviet Central Army in 1976.
(Photo from the Philadelphia Flyers collection)

"We had heard about how they kick and spear, so we stood around waiting for them to do it," said Potvin.

The Flyers weren't as cautious. Sticks, especially those of Ed Van Impe and Andre "Moose" Dupont, were up from the opening face-off. However, it wasn't a stick jab that triggered the stunning walkout by the Soviets at 11:21 of the first period with the score 0-0.

With Van Impe sitting out a hooking penalty, Dupont jolted Alexander Gusev with a body check. Bill Barber thudded into Valeri Vasilyev, then sent leading scorer Valeri Kharlamov crashing into the boards. Moments later, Van Impe left the penalty box, skated directly for Kharlamov in the Flyers' zone and crumpled him to the ice with what was either a charge, elbow or clean check, depending upon who was consulted.

When referee Lloyd Gilmour failed to whistle Van Impe back to the penalty box, then assessed the Soviets a delay-of-game penalty, Coach Konstantim Loktev gestured angrily at Gilmour before waving his team to the dressing room. Most Flyers thought the 18-minute strike was premeditated.

"They were trying to shake us up," said Jimmy Watson. "They should know we're used to pressure. There isn't anything that bothers us."

"I guess they thought they'd upset us," said Orest Kindrachuk. "Well, we took a few shots, then came in here, took off our skates and relaxed. We weren't going anywhere. We live here."

"The delay sure didn't hurt us," said Bobby Clarke. "We scored 20 seconds later." (Reg Leach scored 17 seconds after the unscheduled intermission, deflecting a Bill Barber power-play shot past overworked Soviet goalie Vladislav Tretiak. Meanwhile, the crowd chanted, "Hit 'em again, harder.")

"I didn't think we were that rough," said Clarke. "We just dominated them."

The only Soviet goal was a 40-foot slap shot by Victor Kutyergin that eluded Wayne Stephenson midway in the period. Larry Goodenogh scored the final Flyers' goal at 4:01 of the third period, taking a pass from Clarke during a power-play dash from the right point.

The outcome was decided by then, but Stephenson removed any doubts when he stopped a Boris Mikhalov two-on-one shot with 3:23 to play.

Jimmy Watson, Potvin's All-Star defensive partner, wasn't ready to claim a world championship. But Watson did sum up the Flyers' feelings when he said:

"I think we proved beyond a shadow of a doubt that we're a better club."

Banners reading: "God Bless America, God Save Jewry" and "May We Live in Peace, Let Soviet Jews Live in Peace" were removed before game time when the Soviets objected.

Coach Fred Shero was his usual excitable self: "I feel the same as I did after we beat Boston [for the Stanley Cup]. I don't feel anything now, but I probably will tomorrow."

When board chairman Ed Snider burst through the press delegation to tell Shero "that was the greatest coaching job I've ever seen," Shero smiled and said, "I had a lot of help."

Flyers management chose to play Kate Smith's "God Bless America" rather than the national anthem, as if the emotional crowd and the Flyers needed extra encouragement.

Brian Propp lays a stick on Minnesota North Star Fred Barrett in a
game that took place during the "Streak."
(Photo by George Reynolds)

# FLYERS FIND PLACE IN HISTORY BOOKS

DECEMBER 23, 1979
BY JAY GREENBERG

Pete Peeters was barely outside the locker room door when it began. It started in section J, which has the only view down the tunnel, and spread within seconds until the entire Spectrum was standing as the Flyers hit the ice.

Just where the Flyers' all-time National Hockey League unbeaten streak, which went to 30 last night with a routine 4-2 victory over the Hartford Whalers, stands among the magic moments of sports is, of course, arguable. The pregame press handout noted that the 1971-72 Los Angeles Lakers won 33 in a row. "Will you guys get out of here?" laughed coach Pat Quinn, when it was brought again to his attention. And because this is the NHL and not the NFL or major league baseball, the enormity of what the Flyers have done will never be fully credited.

"Even when we were champions," said Bobby Clarke, "the league was uncomfortable with us. We were the best thing for the sport to come along in years, selling out every building we went into. People love to hate us and instead of taking advantage of it, the league tried to beat us down. They changed rules, they spoke out against us and forced us to change. We probably would have had to change anyway, but they didn't take advantage of a good thing when they had it."

The reason, obviously, was the socially condemnable way the Flyers played. Now that *Newsweek,* which did drop by in the course of the streak, has declared the Flyers to have cleaned up their act, there was no reason to sweep the 1979-80 Flyers' success, of breaking the 29-win streak, under the rug.

"Clarke is still the leader of this team," said winger Paul Holmgren, on the bus on the way to the Boston airport, "and when we saw him downplaying it, we just followed. There's a good reason for it, and it's too early to get pleased with ourselves."

"I don't want to downplay it," said Quinn. "It was a tremendous accomplishment. But it didn't really become a goal until the last few games, when we kept having the number put in front of us.

"You can't say it's the fulfilling of a dream, like the Stanley Cup, because I didn't grow up thinking about what it would be like to set a record. You don't even know what the record is, until someone looks it up. This is platinum. The Stanley Cup is gold."

Because of that, all one can really do is marvel at a hockey team which, one week away from January, has suffered only one loss. And be impressed that the Flyers broke a record set by one of the greatest teams ever to play the sport—the 1977-78 Canadiens. This should help convince the Flyers, who are, in reality, still finding out themselves just how good they can be while they seek their own, more lasting place on a Cup and in history.

But long before the last ovation dies, another one should begin. And should not stop, really, until the Flyers do, lest the enormity of their accomplishment never fully be appreciated.

Defenseman J.J. Daigneault and goalie Ron Hextall
try to swat the puck safely away from the Flyers net.
(Daily News photo by George Reynolds)

# FLYERS STORM BACK AGAIN TO FORCE GAME 7

MAY 28, 1987
BY JAY GREENBERG

We have run out of words before the Flyers have run out of rallies.

They reached the boundaries of imagination several games ago, but that's our limitation, not theirs. A team that prompted legitimate concern whether it had enough legs to survive one round of the playoffs, has arms long enough to have reached right through your heart to within one game of its dreams. And your dreams, too.

"I guess we had a little more to give than what everybody thought," winger Dave Brown said.

It's a child's fantasy, really, winning a Stanley Cup. So it is appropriate that this drive, this absolute refusal to sag under the weight of three substantial leads forged by the greatest offensive machine in NHL history, has taken on a neat mystical sense.

Down, three games to one, headed into Game 5, the Flyers will play Game 7 in Edmonton. Down, 2-0, after 15 minutes in Game 6, they rallied for two third-period goals in the final 6:56 to beat the Oilers, 3-2, and reach the game of their lives.

Brian Propp put one up over Grant Fuhr's glove on a power play to tie it, and 1:24 later, J. J. Daigneault's screened point won it, and the Spectrum walls shook from an earthquake created by the Flyers' heartbeat.

It was magical. It was unbelievable. Maybe the second description short-changed a team that completed its fifth rally from a two-goal deficit in its last 10 games going back to the Montreal series. Ron Hextall should make you believe by now.

Wayne Gretzky, certainly a credible source, said that Hextall was the best goaltender he had ever faced. And of all the rookie goalie's 15 wins in the playoffs, this one, considering the caliber of the competition and the proximity of the ultimate reward, was the most impressive one yet. Hextall was most of what was holding the Flyers in this game for the first 30 minutes.

Goaltending such as this makes anything possible. But the Flyers would have been lined up at center ice congratulating the Oilers on their third Cup in four years had not the improbable taken over from there.

"Miracle" is such an overused term in sports. So is "character." Would you really expect any team as close to the grand prize as the Flyers to pack it in?

"Destiny" is another cliché. Many a team has to believe itself to have it, only to run into the reality of a powerhouse such as the Oilers. All we know for sure about the Flyers' destiny is that they were destined all along to play a seventh game. Winning it? They've got a shot. We'll see.

Flyers goalie Brian Boucher makes one of 57 saves in a five-overtime win against Pittsburgh. (Daily News photo by Yong Kim)

# THE LATE, LATE GLOW

MAY 4, 2000
BY LES BOWEN

Keith Primeau, the guy who got moved from his normal line because he was on the ice for all the Pittsburgh goals in the first two games of the series, became the Flyers' overtime hero around 2:35 a.m.

Primeau cut from the right boards to the right face-off dot with the puck, eluding exhausted Pens defenseman Darius Kasparaitis. Primeau ripped a shot over the shoulder of Penguins goalie Ron Tugnutt, into the short side of the net, just under the crossbar lifting the Flyers to a 2-1 victory.

It was Primeau's first goal of the series, his second of the postseason, 12:01 into the fifth overtime—ending 152 minutes and 1 second worth of hockey, more than two and a half full games. It was the third-longest game in NHL history, the longest since 1936.

"I'd been going wide a lot," Primeau said. "So I crossed [Kasparaitis] up when I pulled it back. Everybody's been on me to shoot the puck more. I guess I got a good one off."

"I knew it was short side," Tugnutt said of the game-winner. "I was thinking hopefully that it just hit the post. When I looked back, I just went numb."

The Flyers come home for Game 5 with the second-round Stanley Cup playoff series tied, 2-2, neither team having yet won at home.

"It's the wildest thing I've ever been through," Tugnutt said. "It's just nuts. People are saying, 'What period is it? Sixth, no eighth.' Your mind is in a daze."

Three minutes and 45 seconds into the fifth OT,

Flyers goalie Brian Boucher made a sparkling glove save on the Pens' Ian Moran. Tugnutt made 70 saves; Boucher made 57.

The first regulation period was like so many in this series for the Flyers—they should have been ahead after 20 minutes, and instead, they trailed, 1-0.

The Flyers kept the pressure on in the second, but they still couldn't score.

The Flyers kept plugging away, and finally, 4:47 into the third, they tied it.

Their snakebitten power play, 0-for-16 in the series, finally got a break. On the face-off following a Martin Straka slashing call, Daymond Langkow won the puck back to Eric Desjardins, who whistled a right-point drive that was going high and wide. Then, somehow, it was in Tugnutt's net.

The Penguins protested, and upstairs, series supervisor Denis Morel painstakingly reviewed the frame-by-frame replay. What it seemed to show was the puck hitting the raised stick of Pens defenseman Bob Boughner, as he jousted in front with John LeClair, then hitting LeClair's helmet before finding the net. But officially, the on-ice ruling of a goal by ref Rob Shick was upheld because the replay was inconclusive, Morel said.

The Flyers had some good chances to win in regulation, but didn't.

"Our guys were really composed [as the overtimes wore on]," Primeau said. "It was really comical. Guys were trying to get pizza. We were trying to figure out which period it was half the time."

Carl Lewis proudly carries the American flag at
the 1984 Summer Olympics in Los Angeles.
(Philadelphia Inquirer photo by John Paul Filo)

# OTHER GREAT SPORTS MEMORIES

Ben Hogan tees off on the 14th hole as Lloyd Mangrum waits
his turn. (Photo from The Philadelphia Inquirer collection)

# HOGAN TAKES OPEN IN GOLF COMEBACK

### JUNE 12, 1950
### BY LANSE MCCURLEY

The long, green fairways of the famous east course at Merion served as a backdrop for one of sport's greatest achievements of heart and strength as Bantam Ben Hogan, so recently within only a short putt of this world's final hole, death, took the greatest club in any golf bag, courage, and blistered the layout with a subpar 69 to win the National Open championship.

He stroked one over par for the first nine and then cut two from regulation figures for a final score of 36-33—69.

Thus, he won the triple playoff for golf's richest prize. His rivals, George Fazio, the pro who learned his game in this section, and Lloyd Mangrum of Illinois, scored 37-38—75, and 36-37—73, respectively.

Mangrum was a threat until the 16th hole, when he picked up his ball from the velvet surface of the green to remove a small bug that had settled annoyingly upon it after a stroke with the putter had failed to move the insect, and was penalized two strokes by the United States Golf Association officials.

From there on, he was through, and the match belonged to the gallant warrior of fairway and green who survived such a terrible automobile accident 16 months ago, they said he would never even play again, let alone figure as a tournament competitor.

His injured legs are still poor of circulation, but his great heart more than compensates. Pain he sank and forgot with each putt, and courage he took from the bag at each tee, and so he walked once again in the high places and won his second Open championship. Mangrum was the 1946 titleholder, and Fazio

was reaching his peak as a competitive golfer among the really greats for the very first time.

But Hogan defeated more than a former Open champion and a possible future one; he defeated tradition and fate and natural law.

On such trivial things as the choice of a landing place by a bug, determined by what forces no one knows, but generally attributed to that plague element called luck, do great championships and great victories sometimes depend.

And yet neither of his rivals gave Hogan anything, and he finished up his tour of the tough course with a skill and precision that would have matched the best of competitors with the greatest of luck. And no one can say that the insect on the ball and the two-stroke penalty made all the difference.

Courage made all the difference, the sort of courage that can discount pain and weariness and see only the star at the end of the glory road and none of the clouds of despair that everyone in every game sooner or later encounters, but only the strong refuse to feel.

Mangrum said after the tournament, "I didn't know the rules nor realize there was a penalty for lifting the ball." Then he added, reflectively and generously but also honestly, "Ben earned it, anyhow."

It was anticlimax, this putt of Mangrum's. The battle was over, the drama had been played and good theater and good sportsmanship demanded a gracious acceptance. Good theater and sportsmanship did not go unheeded. Mangrum bowed to the rules and went right on—so did Hogan, to the championship.

Jimmy Usilton, son of head coach Jim, is front and center for captain
Bill Lindsay and the rest of West Catholic's 1953 city titlists.
(Philadelphia Inquirer photo by Al Deans)

# WEST STOPS STILTS

MARCH 6, 1953
BY STEVE KLESSEL

Coach Jimmy Usilton and player Bill Lindsay were the heroes and West Catholic was the city champion today. Usilton and Lindsay found a way to outscore Overbrook and its 6-foot, 11-inch center, Wilton "Stilts" Chamberlain. The result was a crown-winning 54-42 victory for the Burrs. More than 8,000 watched the contest at the Palestra, with 5,000 more turned away when the fire marshal closed the doors at 5:30, two and a half hours before game time.

Most of the crowd came to see Stilts, one of the most highly publicized players in city scholastic history. But the throng left, marveling not at Stilts, but at the strategy and its execution used to check him.

Chamberlain did not have a bad night. In all, he accounted for 29 points. But the play was taken away from him by Lindsay, who set a new city title game record by netting 32.

For more than half an hour Overbrook had control of the game. At intermission, the Hilltoppers held a 24-20 edge, and at the outset of the third period, widened it to 32-24.

Then they folded up.

With Lindsay a jack-of-all-trades on the court, West dominated the play from that stage on—beginning its rally in an auspicious fashion with eight consecutive points that sent the contest into the final quarter tied at 32.

The continuance of West's spurt turned the game into a rout thereafter.

Lindsay shot from all angles and was constantly able to take the ball from Overbrook when the Hilltoppers had it, and generally stole the entire show from Chamberlain.

However, there was more than Lindsay behind West's victory. There was a master-coaching plan drawn up by Usilton and mainly chosen to stop Chamberlain.

The Burrs' coach, who was winning his second city title in as many seasons, put a tight four-man cordon around the big fellow, and Stilts found it difficult to move without bumping into someone. Perhaps it was this defense more than anything else that captured the decision.

Wilt Chamberlain sails to the basket during his days at Overbrook High School.
(Photo from Daily News collection)

# OVERBROOK STAR ECLIPSES ALL FORMER SCHOOLBOY MARKS

FEBRUARY 17, 1955
BY BILL SHEFSKI

The circular rim is still on the backboard. But those who were on hand to witness the Overbrook-Roxborough Public League basketball game are wondering how it withstood the assault made upon it by Wilt "Stilt" Chamberlain.

Wilton put another leaf into his book of record performances by cracking the state high school scholastic game individual scoring mark of 85 points formerly held by Ray Pauley, Sinking Springs High basketeer, with a 90-point showing, which was more than enough to gain the Hilltoppers their 11th win.

The 7-foot wonder hit on 36 of 41 field goal attempts and 18 of 26 charity tosses, even though he missed four minutes of action in Overbrook's 123-21 win.

In regaining the district mark from Jenkintown's Stodie Watts, who broke Chamberlain's area record of 74 counters on Feb. 1, the Stilt tabbed 64 points in the last half after getting only 26 in the opening 16 minutes.

Chamberlain connected for 31 points in the third period and 33 in the final session for his record-shattering performance.

The 90 points raised the Overbrook lad's season total to 783 tallies, which is a 45.5-per-game average.

Wilt scored 71 against the same team on Jan. 14, 1954, and 74 on Jan. 15 this year for the amazing total of 235 points against the one team.

He has raised his high school career total to 2,089 points, just 133 short of Tom Gola's four-year high of 2,222 which the La Salle College All-American established when he played at La Salle High.

In addition to his top offensive display, Chamberlain played a remarkable defensive game to boot. He took sole control of both backboards and on numerous occasions swatted would-be two-pointers away from the Roxborough basket.

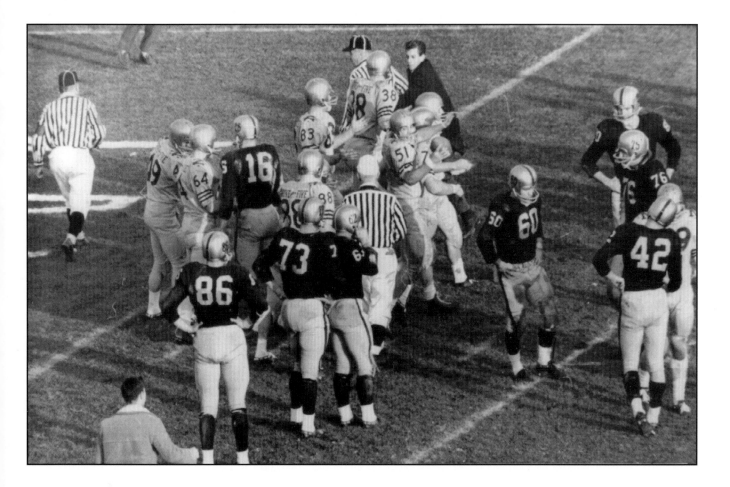

Army and Navy players mill around on the Municipal
Stadium field as time expired in the controversial finish.
(AP/Wide World Photos)

# ARMY–NAVY'S MOST MEMORABLE GAME

### DECEMBER 7, 1963
### BY BILL FLEISCHMAN

---

*This game was selected as the No. 1 game in Army–Navy history and the story was written to commemorate the game's 100th anniversary.*

---

The mood before the game couldn't have been more somber. Imagine playing a football game, even a supercharged Army-Navy game, just more than two weeks after President Kennedy had been assassinated. Kennedy, a Navy veteran of *PT-109* fame, was a devoted Naval Academy football fan. A year earlier, he had participated in the pregame coin toss on the same Municipal Stadium turf where the memorable 1963 game would be played. Before the '63 season, the Navy football team had met the president. His wife, Jacqueline, was returning from a summer vacation in the Mediterranean, and he was meeting her at the Quonset Point naval base in Rhode Island. The Navy team was practicing at the base.

"He arrived about a half hour before she did," recalls linebacker Tom Lynch, the captain of the '63 Navy team. "We were out there in our starchy whites. He came over and spoke with us and signed footballs for us and had pictures taken with him. That reinforced the special affinity we had with John F. Kennedy.

"[His death] was a tremendous blow for everybody in America, but even more so for us because we believed that Kennedy was our guy."

With a nation numb from grief immediately after the assassination, there was talk that the game would be canceled. At the urging of the Kennedy family, however, government officials decided the game would be played a week later than scheduled.

Once the game was on again, the two rivals began to focus on playing. These were two strong teams. Navy, with Heisman Trophy-winning quarterback Roger Staubach, was 8-1 and ranked No. 2 in the nation. Army (7-2) had beaten Penn State, 10-7, and Air Force, 14-10. The winner would be invited to face top-ranked Texas in the Cotton Bowl.

Navy was seeking its fifth consecutive victory over the Cadets. "Drive for Five" was printed on the backs of the Midshipmen's gold uniforms.

"We got ready for the game, then all the emotion was let out," Staubach said from his Dallas office. "It's a little like the Texas A&M tragedy down here. There's the tragedy. Then, all of a sudden, you're in the stadium. There's a lump in your stomach and you want to let out all the pent-up frustration. Everybody is anxious to get playing."

With 100,000 packed into Municipal Stadium (later to be renamed JFK Stadium) on Dec. 7, Navy took a 21-7 lead early in the fourth quarter on Pat Donnelly's third touchdown. It was the only three-TD game of Donnelly's collegiate career. Army then drove 52 yards, with quarterback Rollie Stichweh scoring on a 1-yard plunge. When Stichweh rushed for the two-point conversion, it was Navy 21, Army 15 with 6:19 remaining. As if he hadn't already contributed enough, Stichweh then recovered the onside kickoff at the Navy 49. The Cadets methodically marched to the Navy 4. Halfback Ken Waldrop gained 3 yards to the Navy 1. However, as Army lined up to run another play, time expired.

Coach Jack Friel jumps up during some tense moments in his
North Catholic win. (Philadelphia Inquirer photo by Al Deans)

# NORTH CATHOLIC VARSITY SUSPENDED; JV WALLOPS MCDEVITT

FEBRUARY 26, 1968
BY TOM CUSHMAN

Iggy Brodzinski, Mike Kaiser, Joe Evanosich, Bill Dever, Jim Boylan and the rest of the guys had gathered to have a squad picture snapped for the yearbook. It was the first official meeting of the North Catholic jayvees since their schedule had come to a crushing conclusion eight days earlier. These future Falcons had lost a one-point decision to Father Judge's junior varsity (on a last-second goaltending call) in that final start. The memory was acid, but it was dwarfed by the impending battle between the North varsity and Bishop McDevitt in the Catholic League playoffs. The Falcons are the defending champions, and pride around the school is fierce.

To the jayvees, the playoffs were a basketball oasis, hiding somewhere in the future. At the moment the thrill and the agonies were vicarious, but they would root hard for the varsity. Then, maybe next winter . . . That was when varsity coach Jack Friel suddenly materialized. "Fellows," he said, "you're going down to the Palestra a year early."

With that summons, one of the most remarkable dramas in Catholic League basketball history was under way. The story line had begun to take shape several hours earlier, when the 12 members of North's varsity, runner-up to Judge in the Northern Division's regular-season race, had failed to return to class after being excused from the first period to attend a special Mass. Friel, who also serves as head of discipline for the school, took the matter before the principal, Father Corcoran, and recommended the players be suspended.

"You can imagine what a difficult decision it was," Friel said later. "But one fact stood out above everything else. It was obvious that athletics were being placed in importance ahead of academics, and

that is not the intent of our program. We did what we think was right and just for everyone concerned."

What Friel did was explain to Hank Siemiontkowski, the Catholic League's leading scorer, Joe DeMuro and teammates that they would not be representing the school at the Palestra that evening. At the same time, the jayvees, who had not even been on the practice floor since that afternoon at Father Judge eight days earlier, were told that they would face Bobby Haas, Jim Sullivan and the other gunners in McDevitt's loaded arsenal.

The players were informed at approximately 3:20 p.m. "It didn't allow us much time," Friel said. "We wanted to be down at the Palestra around 6. We did have a 30-minute practice session to check over our offenses. But as far as preparation of a game plan, I told the kids that came under one word . . . hustle."

By the 7 p.m. tip-off, the story, in a myriad of forms, had saturated a Palestra gathering that was to swell to 5,495. Among the humans, there was the temptation to go out for a coffee while the slaughter was effected. They needn't have agonized. Izzy Brodzinski, Mike Kaiser, Joe Evanosich, Bill Dever, Jim Boylan and the rest of the guys stomped on Bishop McDevitt, 77-60. There is no parallel for the accomplishment in Catholic League history. A jayvee team actually defeating a varsity . . . a varsity that had earned a reputation as one of the finest clubs in the area this winter.

At the end, these improbable heroes were wrestled from the scene by a North cheering section that had thundered onto the floor even before the final buzzer. The events of the day had carried them through dismay, to hope, to apprehension and finally to this moment.

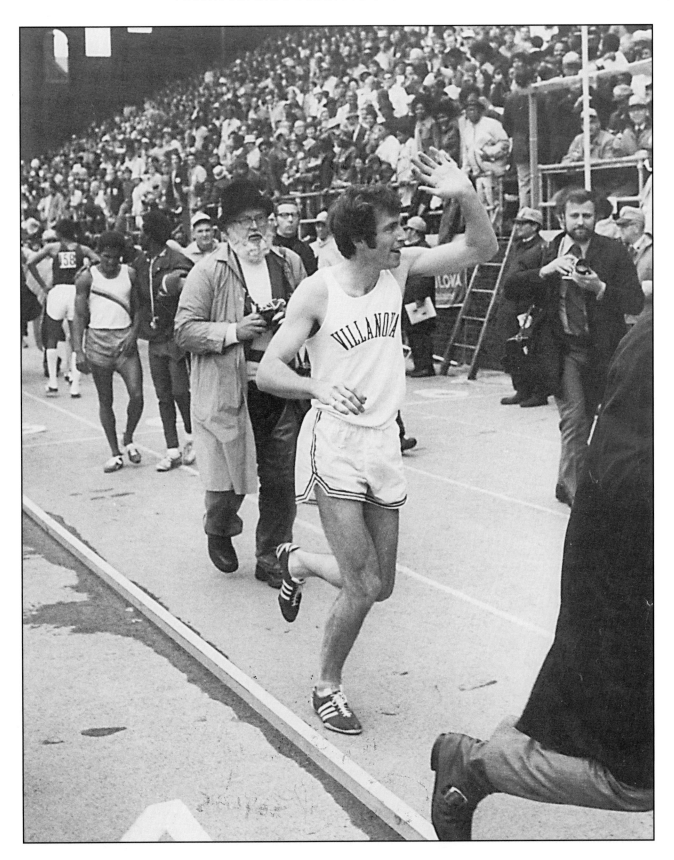

Surrounded by photographers, Marty Liquori waves to
fans after beating Jim Ryun in race at Franklin Field.
(Daily News photo by Sam Psoras)

# LIQUORI WINNER

MAY 16, 1971
BY TOM CUSHMAN

The world of sports, with all of its team standings, volumes of records, exploding scoreboards, gaudy colors and playoffs-to-get-into-playoffs, has never been able to improvise a substitute for the ultimate showdown between two lone men of skill and courage.

With more than 15,000 people straining along with them, Marty Liquori and Jim Ryun plunged into the gloom that hung over Franklin Field and proceeded to brush away the clouds. It took them precisely three minutes, fifty-four and six-tenths seconds to accomplish it.

Liquori won the dream mile, hair streaming, arms upraised in what has become a familiar posture for the greatest middle-distance runner the East has ever produced.

Over an incredible final 600 yards they accelerated, Liquori inviting Ryun to challenge, Ryun responding, Marty holding him off.

It was an even 3:00 at the three-quarters and the remainder of the field had long since been blown out of it.

"Three minutes was no good though," Marty explained. "When I heard that, I thought it was his race. I've never seen anybody who was even with him at 150 yards that didn't get beat.

"I kept waiting for him to come by," Marty said. "I even lost the feeling [in the stretch] of how far we were from the tape. I started to lean one time and we weren't there yet."

Ryun explained that he pulled it all together for the last charge with maybe 100 yards to go. "I saw Marty start to get a bit heavy," he said, "and I figured, 'now'. I moved, then I began to get heavy, too. It was then that I realized how fast we were running."

And that's the way they rolled across the finish line, Liquori never knowing for certain if he was going to hear that "beep-beep" and see Ryun shoot past; Jim that short stride behind as though he were being towed by some invisible line; the crowd in an emotional wringer.

Both were timed in 3:54.6, the fastest mile ever in the East, the fastest ever for Liquori, the fastest for Ryun since he began running again "one year and two days ago."

"If it had been 4:10 and I finished second, I would have been angry with myself," Ryun said. "But it was such a great race, such a fast race, that I'm not disappointed. I'm very pleased with the time, sorry only that I lost."

Liquori, who had started the race on a crescendo of boos, and finished to cheers, brushed aside the significance of the victory as easily as Ryun had the loss. "It was the most exciting mile I've been in in two years," he said. "Other than that, it proves to me I was the best on May 16, nothing more."

Will he be able to get himself as psyched for Jim Ryun on another day?

"If I don't, I'll get beaten," Marty replied, and then a smile spread across his handsome face. "But I could get excited about running against Jim Ryun tomorrow," he added.

You could say he speaks for the world.

The jubilant Overbrook fans celebrate as their team ends West Philadelphia's
winning streak. West Philly's Clarence Tillman (25) can't believe the
scoreboard. (Philadelphia Inquirer photo by Richard M. Titley)

# WEST'S STREAK COMES TUMBLING DOWN

## FEBRUARY 21, 1978
## BY TED SILARY

From the beginning, it was obvious that the Public League basketball happening at Overbrook High would be remembered for years to come, but with just 11 seconds remaining and The 'Brook on top, 60-59, it was not yet clear for what reason.

No one was quite sure whether the game would go down in history as just another victory (albeit with all kinds of excitement) in a West Philadelphia streak that had reached the lofty heights of 68, or whether it would really be the day that the Speedboys came tumbling down.

Only one guy, effervescent Panther point guard Ricky Tucker, could fill in the blanks, and luckily, for cardiac units at hospitals throughout the area, he was not one to dilly-dally as the hearts of an estimated 950 people who had sardined their way into a 700-capacity gym began to pound profusely in syncopated rhythm.

After absorbing a gentle shove near mid-court from All-American Clarence Tillman during a dribbling exhibition that had begun 12 seconds earlier off an inbounds play, Tucker quickly and confidently gave the Speedboys the kind of hard push they had not received since Jan. 24, 1976, by hitting nothing but net on both ends of a one-and-one.

After what seemed like an eternity—which included a basket by West's Kevin McCray at 0:06, a 'Brook time-out at 0:02 and a mid-court interception at 0:01 by Tillman, who never got off a shot—the final count, 62-61, was all but dancing on the scoreboard. And the Panther fans, who had false-started twice already, were all but dancing on the shoulders of their heroes.

That was the way it was when a streak of previously unheard of proportions in hoop-rich Pennsylvania came to an end . . . players hugging fans, fans hugging players, players hugging players, fans hugging fans. And for the first time in a long time, they were not from West Philly.

"All I had to do was step to the line, take a deep breath and let 'em go," said Tucker, who finished with 11 points and countless kisses from female admirers in the mayhem. "I had a long time to think about shooting free throws because I knew I'd have the ball and I knew they'd foul me from the time the ball went out of bounds [at 0:23, as West's Vincent Ross blocked a Tony Costner shot]."

"I feel goooooood," said 6-3 forward Carlton Willis, who totaled a game-high 25 points and a team-high 11 rebounds, getting help from 6-3 guard Carl Lacy (11, 9). "So good I can't even describe it."

West coach Joe Goldenberg and Overbrook's Max Levin left the building with plans for dinner.

"I might even pay for the meal," said Goldenberg, laughing.

"Nah, I think we'll go Dutch," said Levin. "I'll tell you, the fact that I can still be friends with Joey after all the wars we've had on the court is something I really cherish."

Julius Erving congratulates Dobbins Tech's Linda Page at a
Sixers game hours after she scored 100 points in a game.
(Daily News photo by E.W. Faircloth)

# LINDA SCORES 100

FEBRUARY 13, 1981
BY TED SILARY

Dr. Tony Coma, the coach, decided to change his mind; then a star named Linda Page proceeded to rewrite the most noteworthy page in this city's book of schoolperson basketball records.

Remember the days when Wilt Chamberlain, who scored 90 points against Roxborough in February of 1955, held the record for most points scored in a game?

Well, they ended with 4:04 remaining in the fourth quarter of a Public League game between Jules Mastbaum's Tech and host Murrell Dobbins Tech. They ended in a flash, too, as Page, a 5-11 guard, leaped from the right side to follow a missed foul shot by Lisa Gilliam for her 91st and 92nd points.

Better still, with 48 seconds remaining, Page was hacked on a baseline drive and walked to the foul line. Swish. Swish. *One hundred* points.

"I wanted to break Wilt's record, and I'm glad I broke Wilt's record," said Page. "I'm also glad it's over with. Like always, I couldn't have done it without help from my teammates and coach."

It was totally Coma's idea to take another crack at Chamberlain's record.

One month back, after Page had scored 87 points against hapless Roxborough, Doctor Tone promised that "this is the last assault, and nothing will be done on purpose from now on in."

Even before the latest game, he indicated that a film crew from Channel 10 had been invited merely to "capture the hoopla surrounding Linda's 2,000th career point."

Before anyone gets bent out of shape, this was one of the cleanest massacres in basketball history. Dobbins never pressed fullcourt and the starters, except for Page, played no more than half the game.

"Linda Page is a one-in-a-million player," Coma said. "She's a Wilt Chamberlain to the girl's game. I don't care what people think about me. But I do care about Linda Page. I want people to know: she's a great player."

Page reached 37 points and the 2,000 mark on a breakaway layup (pass from Freda Harris) with 4:51 remaining in the second quarter. Her quarter-by-quarter scoring breakdown was 27-26-27-20.

"I enjoyed this game more than the other one [Roxborough]," Linda said. "Why? I was making more of my shots.

"Really, this wasn't planned. It just started as the day to hit 2,000. But I got 37 pretty quick, and I knew by the half that I had to be close to 50. We could see that the record was within reach."

Yes. One hundred. Wilt would never believe it.

Carl Lewis takes the baton from U.S. teammate Calvin Smith as
the two help the United States to a gold medal in the 4 x 100-
meter relay at the 1984 Summer Olympics in Los Angeles.
(AP/Wide World Photos)

# LEWIS SEES NEW WORLDS TO CONQUER

AUGUST 11, 1984
BY MARK WHICKER

They had remarked upon his passion for fashionable tardiness, so Carl Lewis was seven minutes early.

They had burned over his silence during competition, so Carl Lewis was chatty and friendly and forthright for 45 minutes. And said practically nothing.

It was not true that Carl Lewis controlled this Olympics; the Games were far too big even for him. But, as promised, Lewis maintained the same unrelenting grip on himself and everything that involved him.

The world record that everyone had requested of Lewis finally came, on a warm, poignant Saturday afternoon at the Los Angeles Memorial Coliseum.

Lewis ran what was estimated as an 8.94 100 from a running start, with no one pushing, and finished the work of the U.S. 4 x 100 relay team in 37.83, which no one had ever done.

But the crowd, the people? They are drawn to Carl Lewis as they are rarely drawn to anyone who does not play professional team sport in this country. Five minutes after the relay, you could walk through a Coliseum tunnel and into the concourses and swear you were in another land. There were 88,000 people in the Coliseum. At that moment, none of them was hungry or thirsty. The concession stands were empty. No lines. And, for a moment, no one stood taking pictures of the torch.

Carl Lewis kept them in their seats. He had given them his all. The Coliseum housed track-and-field for seven days. He performed on six of those days. He also had to win.

He also rated the four golds a higher feat than winning a decathlon, "because I had to keep preparing myself for a longer period of time. The decathlon is two days. If you get a sore muscle, you run it out and you're ready to go to the next event. I get a sore muscle, I run it out and then I have to go again the next time. Mentally, it also was tougher. It's a joy, but a relief, to have it over."

When he ran with the flag after the 100 meters, it looked as if he had practiced it for months. When he listened to media questions, a look of recognition crossed his face about halfway through each one, and you could see him pushing the buttons on the terminal inside his head. He prefaced every answer with "OK," as if that were his starter's gun.

It was with that studied sincerity that Lewis issued the following thoughts: He would now try to break the long-jump record if it is convenient. "Since I'm not trying to win four events, I think I'll concentrate on the long jump and the 200. World records do mean an awful lot," he said. "But the victories in these Games mean more."

He teased with the thought of playing for the Dallas Cowboys. Asked what it would take, he turned to his business manager, Joe Douglas, and said, "Answer this one, Joe. And be serious this time." Douglas merely said it would take a lot of money. Of course, Lewis probably would want to play quarterback.

Spend A Buck is clearly ahead of Creme Fraiche
at the finish line of the Jersey Derby.
(AP/Wide World Photos/George Widman)

# A CHAMPION'S HEART

MAY 27, 1985
BY STAN HOCHMAN

Spend A Buck won the Kentucky Derby by five lengths in the third-fastest time in the whole cockeyed history of the race, by the biggest margin in 30 years, after the swiftest mile in 111 runnings. After the race was over, after jockey Angel Cordero  punched a glorious hole in the Kentucky sunshine with his fist, trainer Cam Gambolati saw something more remarkable.

"I didn't see it until I looked at the replays," Gambolati gurgled after another big win, yesterday's Jersey Derby. "They were showing the Kentucky Derby over and over again until I saw it. The gameness everybody wondered about. After the race, Cordero is trying to pull him up. He's galloping out, his ears are pricked. Two horses come alongside. It took 'em a half mile to catch up.

"And then, the reins went from dangling to tough, and Angel couldn't pull him up. The outrider with the microphone came alongside to get some quotes and Angel waves her away, because he can't pull the horse up. He wasn't going to let anyone pass him, even then.

"I wanted Lafitt Pincay, Spend A Buck's jockey at the Jersey Derby, to see that. So, we went into the publicity office and looked at the tapes of his last three races. I showed Pincay what happened after the Derby and I told him 'There's gameness there everybody don't know about.'"

Everybody knows about it now. Everybody knows that Spend A Buck has a heart as big as Mount Everest and just as rugged.

Spend A Buck earned $2.6 million for owner Dennis Diaz, a purse of $600,000 and a $2 million bonus for winning the Cherry Hill Mile, Garden State Stakes, Kentucky Derby and Jersey Derby.

"It was," Pincay said later, "the toughest race I can remember for a long time. Go the first part so fast, and then one horse comes at you inside, another one outside."

"It was," Gambolati said with a sigh, "the longest 2 minutes and 2 seconds of my life."

"It was," Diaz said, running out of poetry, "a great race."

The gates clanged open and Spend A Buck toppled out, awkward, off-balance, the ground turning to crumbly dust beneath his front feet.

Purple Mountain, thrashing out of the gate to his left, careened into Spend A Buck's left hip, jolting him off stride, putting a gash above his left rear ankle.

Spend A Buck, startled, put his head down. Pincay yanked it up. The horse would return from this incredible journey with his tongue cut and bleeding. It probably happened just a few strides out of the gate.

Later on, they poked around inside him with a sharp stick and found out what he was made of.

"Guts," said Mr. William Farish, Kentucky breeder, Jockey Club official and host to the Queen of England.